The North Korean Refugee Crisis:

Human Rights and International Response

edited by Stephan Haggard and Marcus Noland

Contributors:
- **Yoonok Chang**
- **Joshua Kurlantzick**
- **Andrei Lankov**
- **Jana Mason**

U.S. Committee for Human Rights in North Korea

Copyright © 2006 by the U.S. Committee for Human Rights in North Korea
All rights reserved.

Printed in the United States of America.

All illustrations copyright © by Citizens' Alliance for North Korean Human Rights.
Reprinted with permission.

ISBN 0-9771-1111-3

Library of Congress Control Number: 2006934326

The North Korean Refugee Crisis:
Human Rights and International Response

U.S. Committee for Human Rights in North Korea
1025 F Street, NW
Suite 800
Washington, DC 20004 USA

Designed by Stewart Andrews, Noodlebox Design, LLC

The U.S. Committee for Human Rights in North Korea is an independent, nongovernmental organization based in Washington, D.C. Created in 2001, the Committee was established to conduct independent research on human rights abuses in North Korea, and to disseminate its findings. It is not affiliated with the U.S. government.

Board of Directors

Morton Abramowitz, *The Century Foundation*

Jaehoon Ahn, *Radio Free Asia*

Richard V. Allen, *The Richard V. Allen Company*

Lisa Colacurcio, *UBS*

Rabbi Abraham Cooper, *The Simon Wiesenthal Center*

John Despres, *Aristotle International*

Chuck Downs, *author of* Over the Line: North Korea's Negotiating Strategy

Nicholas Eberstadt, *American Enterprise Institute*

Phil Fishman, *consultant*

Gordon Flake, *The Maureen and Mike Mansfield Foundation*

Carl Gershman, *National Endowment for Democracy*

Helen-Louise Hunter, *author of* Kim Il-song's North Korea

Fred Iklé, *Center for Strategic and International Studies*

Steve Kahng, *4C Ventures*

Thai Lee, *Software House International*

James Lilley, *American Enterprise Institute*

Andrew Natsios, *Georgetown University*

Jack Rendler, *Human rights advocate*

Suzanne Scholte, *North Korea Freedom Coalition*

Stephen J. Solarz, *APCO Worldwide*

Advisory Council

Gary Ackerman, *U.S. House of Representatives*

Mark Kirk, *U.S. House of Representatives*

Helie Lee, *author of* In the Absence of Sun: A Korean American Woman's Promise to Reunite Three Lost Generations of Her Family

Joseph Pitts, *U.S. House of Representatives*

Samantha Power, *Harvard University*

John Shattuck, *John F. Kennedy Library Foundation*

Debra Liang-Fenton, *Executive Director*
U.S. Committee for Human Rights in North Korea
1025 F Street, NW, Suite 800
Washington, DC 20004 USA
Tel: (202) 378-9579
Fax: (202) 378-9407
Web: WWW.HRNK.ORG

Editors

Stephan Haggard is Lawrence and Sallye Krause Professor at the Graduate School of International Relations and Pacific Studies at the University of California, San Diego, where he serves as Director of the Korea-Pacific Program.

Marcus Noland is a Senior Fellow at the Institute for International Economics.

Contributors

Yoonok Chang is a human rights researcher and a professor at Hansei University, South Korea.

Joshua Kurlantzick is a Visiting Scholar in the China Program at the Carnegie Endowment for International Peace.

Andrei Lankov is a Lecturer on the faculty of Asian Studies at the China and Korea Center at Australian National University. He is on-leave teaching at Kookmin University, Seoul, South Korea.

Jana Mason is a lawyer who has worked on refugee issues for more than 20 years. She is currently with a humanitarian relief organization, and has a particular focus on the Asia region.

Acknowledgments

This report is the culmination of the prodigious efforts of a group of dedicated individuals. The U.S. Committee for Human Rights in North Korea is indebted to researchers Yoonok Chang, Joshua Kurlantzick, Andrei Lankov, and Jana Mason for their hard work and thoughtful analyses. The Committee is particularly grateful to the report's editors, Stephan Haggard and Marcus Noland, whose innumerable contributions to this project have been truly invaluable. The Committee thanks the anonymous reader and the reader who chose to relinquish anonymity, Courtland Robinson, for their insightful comments. Daniel Pinkston, Erik Weeks, Eric Kramon, Baya Harrison, and Ashley Kang provided important assistance. There are many others who informed content and gave assistance to the Committee and to the report's researchers. For their contributions, the Committee is extremely grateful.

Regarding the Illustrations

The illustrations in this report were produced by Hyok Kang. Born in 1986 in North Hamgyong province in North Korea, he escaped from North Korea by crossing the Tumen River with his parents in March 1998. He made the drawings in 2003. His book recounting his experiences in North Korea is called, *"Ici, C'est le paradis!" Une enfance en Coree du Nord ["Here, It Is Paradise!" A Childhood in North Korea]* with Philippe Grangereau (Michel Lafon, 2004). Mr. Kang's testimony may be found at http://www.nkhumanrights.or.kr/NKHR_new/inter_conf/Hyok_Kang.html. The Committee is grateful to Mr. Kang and to the Citizens' Alliance for North Korean Human Rights for their contributions to this project.

Table of Contents

Preface 7
Richard V. Allen and Stephen J. Solarz

Introduction: The North Korean Refugees as a Human Rights Issue 9
Stephan Haggard and Marcus Noland

North Korean Refugees in China: Evidence from a Survey 14
Yoonok Chang, with Stephan Haggard and Marcus Noland

    Table 1. Occupation of Sample 16
    Table 2. Education of Sample 16
    Table 3. Original Residence in North Korea 17
    Figure 1. Map of North Korea 17
    Table 4. Sources of Information on China 20
    Table 5. Sources of Help in Leaving North Korea 20
    Table 6. Length of Time in China 21
    Table 7. Current Residence 21
    Table 8. Reasons for Returning to North Korea 22
    Table 9. Country of Preference 22
    Table 10. Reported Price of North Korean Brides in China 23
    Table 11. Post-Traumatic Stress Disorder Indicators 25
    Table 12. Mean of Psychological Distress 25
    Table 13. Reasons for Anxiety 25
    Table 14. Sentiments about the Government 27
    Table 15. Primary Food Sources in North Korea 28
    Table 16. Improvement of Food Shortage in the Last Two Years 28
    Table 17. North Koreans Are Voicing Their Concerns about Chronic Food Shortages 29

    References 31

    Appendix
    Table 1. Occupational Status of Respondents and Parents 33

North Korean Refugees: The Chinese Dimension 34
Joshua Kurlantzick and Jana Mason

Bitter Taste of Paradise: North Korean Refugees in South Korea 53
Andrei Lankov

    Table 1. Number of Newly Arrived North Korean Defectors to the South 54

Conclusions 73
Stephan Haggard and Marcus Noland

Preface
Richard V. Allen and Stephen J. Solarz

When we consider North Korea these days, our thoughts turn to the unpleasant prospect of an isolated regime, virtually owned and operated by an unusual, reclusive leader and his coterie of well-armed and determined militarists, acquiring a substantial nuclear weapons capacity, potentially selling fissile material or even nuclear weapons to terrorist groups or rogue regimes, and possibly launching a war of cataclysmic proportions by accident or by design. This is a great problem, one of many, confronting the world.

Comparatively little is known about North Korea's internal mechanisms, yet it has a weighty and disproportionate presence in the broad array of policy problems facing its neighbors, especially Japan and China, and, by extension, the United States. North Korea operates a thriving weapons export program, including missiles, it remains on the terrorist list produced by the U.S. Department of state, it counterfeits American currency, sells illegal drugs and fake cigarettes, all to gain foreign exchange. Yet it cannot and does not feed its own population, and in the past has resorted to starvation as a political instrument.

Concentration on the strategic problem in the national security context is clearly warranted, yet there is another, growing dimension to the North Korean problem that poses a grave challenge: the plight of ordinary North Koreans who are denied even the most basic human rights, and the dramatic and heart-rending stories of those who risk their lives in the struggle to escape what is certainly the world's worst nightmare, the tyranny of the Kim Jong Il regime. These refugees take the risk for various reasons, such as persecution and severe hunger, but all believe that life "on the other side" will be better, and will provide opportunities that will never come if they remain.

In many refugee situations, "escape" does mean the chance to start over, and by dint of hard work, sacrifice and keeping a vision of a brighter future, individuals can and do succeed. Successful escape from North Korea, however, can mean that the refugee may merely be trading one prison for another, as this important new study by the Committee clearly demonstrates.

In this report, six experts—Stephan Haggard, Marcus Noland, Yoonok Chang, Joshua Kurlantzick, Jana Mason and Andrei Lankov—examine in convincing detail the plight of those determined escapees and the extraordinary problems they face once they have cleared what becomes only the preliminary hurdle of crossing the border.

There is a delicate web of competing and often conflicting interests affecting the future of the North Korean refugees. For its part, China, despite its legitimate interests in preventing a massive inflow of North Koreans in its long common border region, fails to meet its international obligations as a signatory to the United Nations Convention on Human Rights. The present study demonstrates convincingly that China is inhospitable to the refugees in many ways, including detention, allowing forced repatriation, and turning a blind eye to trafficking in women, for whom an average price of less than $250 can mean subjugation, abuse, or a life of forced prostitution. In China, refugees are exploited, live in permanent fear of the severe penalties they face if repatriated or those available in China if they are apprehended.

The Republic of Korea, for its part, has adopted what Stephan Haggard and Marcus Noland identify as a "shamefully ambivalent" attitude, despite affecting a "one Korea" policy stance as enshrined in the ROK Constitution.

The U.S. Committee for Human Rights in North Korea, now in its fifth year, has previously published important studies on "*The Hidden Gulag: Exposing North Korea's Prison Camps*" (2003) and "*Hunger and Human Rights: The Politics of Famine in North Korea*" (2005), and now presents this important new study on the plight of North Korean refugees in China and South Korea, offering remedies for one of the world's most pressing problems.

We commend it to the attention of the general reader as well as to specialists in the hope of drawing closer attention to the urgent need for action.

Richard V. Allen

Stephen J. Solarz

Introduction

The North Korean Refugees as a Human Rights Issue

Stephan Haggard and Marcus Noland

North Korea typically enters the news through the lens of high politics and security. However, North Korea poses a host of human rights and humanitarian challenges as well, including well documented abuses of the most fundamental human rights and civil liberties, the maintenance of an elaborate Soviet-style gulag, the suppression of religion, and ongoing politically-derived problems of food security.[1]

To these must be added the problem of North Korean refugees, most of whom reside in China.[2] There are at least three reasons why the refugee issue must be viewed through a human rights prism:

- The first is that the flow of refugees stems in no small measure from human rights abuses in North Korea. Refugees are motivated strongly by economic deprivation in North Korea. But as other work by the Committee has shown, the economic collapse of the mid-1990s, the famine and, ongoing food shortages cannot be disentangled from fundamental features of the regime itself. Moreover, as Joshua Kurlantzick and Jana Mason argue forcefully in their contribution to this report, economic motivations do not relieve the international community of its obligations to these refugees, particularly when they are treated as political refugees by the sending country and subject to punishment for defection if they return.

- Second, the North Korean refugees raise human rights questions because of their treatment in the countries to which they initially flee, and most notably in China. As the contribution by Yoonok Chang shows, the very vulnerability of the refugees makes them subject to a variety of abuses including those perpetrated by employers, brokers, and individuals engaged in outright human trafficking.

- The third and final component of the human rights problem of the refugees concerns the obligations of the international community with respect to their ultimate domicile. North Korean refugees have managed to escape through China and reach Russia, Southeast Asia, and other destinations. Their treatment has been far from uniform, and in many cases they have been left dangling in a political and diplomatic limbo: unable to return to their home country because of conditions there; unable to stay where they are; yet also unable to move on. In the conclusion to this report, the nature of the American obligation in this regard is addressed.

China faces a number of difficult policy dilemmas with respect to North Korea, of which the refugee problem is only one. As Americans should well understand, a porous border and large income differentials are ample cause for population flows that can pose acute social challenges. Nonetheless, any sympathy we may have for the policy challenges faced by Beijing does not excuse maltreatment of refugees in the countries to which they flee. Nor does it relieve China—or any other country—from its obligations under existing international agreements, including most notably the United Nations Refugee Convention discussed in detail by Kurlantzick and Mason.

---

[1] On the general human rights situation, see KINU (2006). On the North Korean gulag see Hawk (2003). On food security see Amnesty International (2004), and Haggard and Noland (2005, 2007). On religion see Hawk (2005).

[2] See, for example, Human Rights Watch (2002), Refugees International (2005), and Lee (2006), and International Crisis Group (2006).

South Korea's obligations are also particularly complex because of the divided nature of the peninsula. Nonetheless, as Andrei Lankov shows in his contribution, both the South Korean government and the public at large are rethinking their posture toward refugees, and in ways that will pose additional human rights challenges in the future. If South Korea becomes more cautious about taking refugees, even at the margin, then the obligations of other countries will need to adjust accordingly. Clearly, a coordinated response to the North Korean refugee problem would be the most desirable outcome.

This report begins with the contribution by Yoonok Chang that draws on a survey conducted on the Chinese border to paint a picture of the refugee community in China. The report then turns to the policy dilemmas facing China, and considers how China's management of the refugee issue to date fits within its larger foreign policy toward North Korea and its international obligations. Finally, the report closes with a contribution by Andrei Lankov that considers the difficulties North Korean refugees face in South Korea. His account, which emphasizes the tremendous difficulty of integrating North Koreans into a market-oriented democratic polity, is a telling reminder of the long-run costs posed by regimes that violate fundamental human rights.

North Koreans in China

Refugee interviews are an important source of information both on North Korea itself and on conditions among the refugees in China. A team lead and trained by Yoonok Chang interviewed a total of 1,346 refugees at nine locations in China in late 2004 and early 2005, representing a wide cross-section of the refugee community. Her contribution to this collection documents the findings of this survey.

The report describes, first, who the refugees are and provides evidence on why and how they left North Korea, their living conditions in China, and their future intentions: whether they intend to remain in China, return to North Korea, or migrate on to a third-country destination. Not surprisingly, economic calculations dominate their reasons for leaving North Korea. Although there is some evidence among younger refugees of movement back and forth across the border, most envision themselves as residing in China on a temporary basis before moving on to a third country, typically South Korea.

The survey highlights the multiple sources of vulnerability in the refugee community in China, including not only fear of arrest, but also the uncertainty of their work circumstances and the particular vulnerability of women to various forms of abuse and outright trafficking. The Chang survey is unique in considering not only the objective conditions of the refugees but their psychological state as well. Not surprisingly, refugees suffer from anxiety and depression associated with the uncertainty of their circumstances as well as the loss associated with their severed ties with North Korea. Their symptoms are not unlike post-traumatic stress disorder.

Refugee interviews have been an important source of information on North Korea, and the Chang survey posed a number of questions about conditions there. The timing of the survey is of particular interest because a number of the refugees had direct experience with the economic reforms introduced by the government in the summer of 2002. As the survey results show, the effects of these reforms were mixed at best and resentment toward the North Korean leadership for the continued hardship in the country is high.

The survey also provides revealing information on the foreign-aid effort. Since the famine of the mid-1990s, the humanitarian community has poured over $1.5 billion in food aid into the country; at its peak, the foreign-aid effort was feeding as much as one-third of the entire population of the country (Haggard and Noland 2005). Nonetheless, the government has effectively disguised this effort. Few North Koreans are aware of the magnitude of foreign aid, and most think that aid is diverted to the military.

Looking ahead, what is surprising about this group of refugees is their optimism in the face of adversity. Despite harsh conditions, these refugees maintain the hope that their status will be regularized or that they will be able to fit in or transit from China to a better future.

The Chinese Dimension

The contribution by Kurlantzick and Mason explores the Chinese dimension of the refugee problem, beginning with a detailed examination of the UN Refugee Convention. They argue that any North Korean who has fled to China should have *prima facie* claim to refugee status. This status is based on the likelihood of being persecuted for having exercised the fundamental right—recognized in international human rights law—to leave one's country. They argue that this obligation is unaffected by the fact that many North Koreans—as Chang shows—leave for economic reasons. The motives of refugees are mixed and complex, and encompass economic, political, and social factors. However, these mixed motives do not disqualify an individual from refugee protection, particularly if they face persecution upon their return.

The People's Republic of China has been a member of the Executive Committee of the High Commissioner's Program (ExCom) since 1958 and became a party to the Convention in 1982, albeit subject to some reservations. China has not enacted specific legislation to codify its obligations under the Refugee Convention and administers no national refugee adjudication process. However, since 1986 it has allowed those seeking asylum for political reasons to reside in China following a review of their status. China has permitted asylum seekers to openly approach the UN High Commissioner for Refugees (UNHCR) office in Beijing, to receive refugee status determination from the UNHCR, and to remain in China pending resettlement. North Koreans are explicitly excluded from this process, however, despite the fact that UNHCR and nongovernmental organizations (NGOs) would gladly assist them and South Korea is willing—at least in principle—to take them.

That China is violating its international obligations toward North Korean refugees and asylum seekers in its territory is not news to refugee or human rights advocates. But the North Korean refugee crisis has often—and rightly—been called a "hidden" refugee crisis because China has succeeded in preventing what would otherwise be a massive international response in the form of assistance and protection. It would not be hard to imagine hundreds of thousands of North Korean refugees in UNHCR-administered camps in Northeast China, with NGOs carrying out their traditional assistance roles while an international resettlement effort—perhaps along the lines of the Vietnamese resettlement model—was underway. Of course, while this is neither the only—nor necessarily even the most likely—outcome, the issue of how best to handle China with respect to its obligations is a crucial one, and an issue that is addressed in the conclusion of the report.

North Koreans in the South

Discussions of the North Korean refugee problem have quite naturally focused on the difficulties facing those living in China. Yet as Chang shows in her paper, most of these refugees would prefer to live elsewhere, primarily in South Korea, and a small but growing community of North Korean refugees currently lives there. Their experience provides insight into the problems of absorbing refugees from a country such as North Korea, with its long isolation from international contact and peculiar social and educational institutions. The problems of absorbing North Korean refugees are not trivial, as both the South Korean government and the public at large are learning.

The report by Andrei Lankov considers the history of the North Korean defector community in South Korea, its interaction with South Korean society and changing official and non-official responses to the defectors. In the past, most defectors came from privileged groups in the North Korean population, and their adjustment to the new environment did not pose significant challenge. However, from the mid-1990s onward, defectors began to come from far less privileged groups, and now this community much more closely resembles the composition of the North Korean populace. If anything, geographically or socially disadvantaged groups are overrepresented among the refugees. Not surprisingly, these refugees face problems in finding and holding work, with education, with crime, and a more general social malaise.

This changing composition of the defector community has not escaped the attention of South Korean officials and analysts, and the political utility of defectors has fallen. Recent years have seen a dramatic, but not always openly stated, change in the official South Korean attitude toward defectors: from a policy explicitly aimed at encouraging defection, Seoul has moved to the policy of quietly discouraging it. There are two reasons for such a new approach. First are the fears that encouraging defection will undermine the policy of peaceful engagement with the North. But increasingly, the perception is growing that refugees are outsiders who face insurmountable difficulties in adjusting to the conditions of South Korean society.

This change in perception—from fellow countrymen in need of help to unwanted burden—has important implications not only for the refugees but also for South Korean strategy toward the North more generally. Changing views toward refugees help explain the broad support for a strategy of political engagement with North Korea, but also pose challenges for the international effort to address the problem of North Korean refugees.

Conclusions

The analysis presented in this report has important implications for international and U.S. policy, upon which the conclusion elaborates. Recent changes to U.S. asylum law require that a "central motive" for persecution must be one of the five Convention grounds: race, religion, nationality, social group, and political opinion. But the Convention itself places no such burden on the asylum seeker to parse the motives of the persecutor in such a manner; the United States—no less than China—has obligations under the Convention. The North Korea Human Rights Act (NKHRA) takes modest steps in ameliorating this situation. The legislation clarifies that North Koreans should not be barred from eligibility for refugee or asylum status in the United States due to any legal claim they may have to South Korean citizenship. It calls on the state Department to facilitate the submission of applications by North Koreans seeking protection as refugees. Finally, the bill authorizes up to $20 million for humanitarian assistance for North Koreans outside of North Korea.

The first concrete outcome of this legislation occurred in May 2006, when the U.S. government admitted six North Koreans to the United States as refugees. While a significant development, it was not—as many proponents of the legislation have claimed—made possible only through the NKHRA. The North Koreans, who were processed in a Southeast Asian country, were admitted through the U.S. refugee admissions program established under the Refugee Act of 1980. The NKHRA nonetheless constituted an important message from the Congress to the state Department and others within the administration that the issue of North Korean refugees needed to be addressed in a more vigorous way.

U.S. government policy does not have to end there, however. Most refugees would prefer to live in South Korea, and it is reasonable to assume that most of those who make it out of China will ultimately settle there. The United States has extensive experience with refugee resettlement and with the challenges of integrating refugees from different backgrounds into the host country's culture. Technical cooperation with South Korea could be a beneficial first step to addressing this issue, and could be particularly important during a period in which the political relationship between the two capitals appears to be under some strain. However, it would constitute only a first step that would also have to include a strategy for discussing the obligations of China and other countries toward this particularly disadvantaged group.

References

Amnesty International. 2004. *Starved of Rights: Human Rights and the Food Crisis in the Democratic People's Republic of Korea (North Korea)*. New York: Amnesty International.

Haggard, Stephan and Marcus Noland. 2005. *Hunger and Human Rights: The Politics of Famine in North Korea*. Washington: U.S. Committee for Human Rights in North Korea.

Haggard, Stephan and Marcus Noland. 2007. *Famine in North Korea: Markets, Aid, and Reform*. New York: Columbia University Press.

Hawk, David. 2003. *The Hidden Gulag: Exposing North Korea's Prison Camps Prisoners' Testimonies and Satellite Photographs*. Washington: U.S. Committee for Human Rights in North Korea.

Hawk, David. 2005. *Thank You, Father Kim Il-Sung: Eyewitness Accounts of Severe Violations of Freedom of Thought, Conscience, and Religion in North Korea*. Washington: United States Commission on International Religious Freedom.

Human Rights Watch. 2002. *The Invisible Exodus: North Koreans in the People's Republic of China*. New York: Human Rights Watch.

International Crisis Group. 2006. *Perilous Journeys: The Plight of the North Korean Refugees in China and Beyond."* Asia Report No. 122. October 26, at <http://www.crisisgroup.org/home/index.cfm?id=4469&l=1>.

KINU. 2006. *White Paper On Human Rights in North Korea*. Seoul: Korea Institute for National Unification.

Lee, Keumsoon. 2006. "The Border-crossing North Koreans: Current Situations and Future Prospects," *Studies Series* 06-05. Seoul: Korea Institute for National Unification.

Refugees International. 2005. *Acts of Betrayal: the Challenge of Protecting North Koreans in China*. Washington: Refugees International.

North Korean Refugees in China: Evidence from a Survey

Yoonok Chang
with Stephan Haggard and Marcus Noland

Famine, continuing food shortages, and political repression in North Korea have driven tens of thousands of people to cross the border into China's northeastern provinces. The precise number having made this journey remains uncertain; estimates range from 20,000 to as high as 400,000.[1] Although the high end of this range probably exaggerates the numbers currently in China (Refugees International 2005, 5-6), the plight of these refugees has only become more precarious over time. Chinese surveillance of the border region has intensified since 2001 as part of a nationwide "Strike Hard" campaign against social deviance, and following a number of incidents in which North Koreans entered and occupied foreign embassies and consulates in order to seek shelter and asylum in 2002. These episodes were followed by the forcible repatriation of tens of thousands of North Koreans by the Chinese authorities.

The refugee situation is of interest for at least two reasons. The first and most obvious is humanitarian concern about the conditions of the refugees themselves. But the refugees' motivations and experiences documented in this study provide a remarkable window into life in North Korea as well.

The study was conducted from August 2004 to September 2005 by 48 individuals trained by the author before conducting the interviews. Because of the changed conditions on the border, conducting such interviews has become much more difficult, if not altogether impossible, since that time. Many refugees were suspicious and refused to answer on paper, and in these cases, the responses were memorized by the interviewers to dissipate this anxiety.[2] A total of 1,346 refugees were ultimately interviewed in Shenyang, Changchun, Harbin, Yangbin, Tumen, Helong, Hunchun, Dandong, Jilin, Tonghua, and Wangqing. We do not claim that they constitute a random sample, which would be impossible to frame. Nonetheless, these interviews broadly reflect the characteristics of the North Korean refugee population and constitute an important window onto their current status.

The study is organized as follows. The first section outlines the nature of the sample. Who are the refugees? How representative are they of the North Korean population? Are there reasons to believe that their attitudes or experiences may be systematically biased or distinct?

The second section focuses on the reasons why refugees left North Korea, their living conditions in China, and their future intentions: whether they intend to remain in China, return to North Korea, or migrate on to a third-country destination. As we will see, despite the precariousness of their status and their preference for a decent life in North Korea, few plan on returning. Most envision themselves as residing in China on a temporary basis before moving on to a third country. Yet there is evidence of considerable movement back and forth across the border, mostly people carrying money and food back to their extended family members in North Korea.

---

[1] See Lee (2006:18-19) for a summary of alternative estimates.

[2] To avoid interviewing the same individuals, the refugees were not paid for doing interviews. Given the use of multiple interviewers over an extended period of time, however, the possibility of a single individual being interviewed more than once cannot be categorically excluded. In the case of Shenyang, interviews were conducted on two separate occasions. The identities of the respondents in the first set of interviews were recorded, and these individuals were excluded from the second round of interviews.

The survey sheds light on the multiple sources of vulnerability in the refugee community in China. These include not only fear of arrest, but also the uncertainty of their work circumstances and the particular vulnerability of women to forms of abuse such as trafficking.

In the fourth section, this analysis of objective conditions extends to a consideration of the psychology of the refugees. This human dimension of the refugee's plight is a recurrent theme in refugee testimony. This study finds, not surprisingly, that refugees suffer from anxiety and depression associated with past traumas, the uncertainty of their circumstances, and the loss of ties with North Korea.

Refugee interviews have been an important source of information on North Korea, and the survey posed a number of questions about conditions there. The timing of the survey is of particular interest because a number of the refugees had direct experience of the economic reforms introduced by the government in the summer of 2002. As the survey results show, the effects of these reforms were mixed at best and resentment toward the North Korean leadership for the continued hardship in the country is high.

The survey also provides revealing information on the foreign-aid effort. Since the famine of the mid-1990s, the humanitarian community has poured over $1.5 billion in food aid into the country; at its peak, the foreign-aid effort was feeding as much as one-third of the entire population of the country (Haggard and Noland 2005). Nonetheless, the government has effectively disguised this effort. Few North Koreans are aware of the magnitude of foreign aid, and most think that aid is diverted to the military.

Looking ahead, what is surprising about this group of refugees is their optimism in the face of adversity. Despite harsh conditions, these refugees maintain the hope that their status will be regularized or that they will be able to fit in or transit from China to a better future. These findings carry an obligation for the international community: to help make these hopes a reality by continuing to focus attention on their plight.

Who Are the Refugees?

Large numbers of refugees first began crossing into China in the mid- to late-1990s as North Korea slipped into famine and central control began to fray, particularly in the northeastern provinces bordering China. There is some evidence that the numbers of border crossings have declined in more recent years as the worst of the famine passed, and both China and North Korea increased security on the border.

Males made up a majority of those early border-crossers, but in more recent years women have come to predominate. Our survey reflects this phenomenon: women make up a slight majority (52 percent) of the respondents. Not surprisingly, prime-age adults, between the ages of 25 and 50, account for nearly four-fifths of those surveyed.

In the late 1980s, the government divided the labor force into four categories: "workers," who were employed at state-owned enterprises; "farmers," who worked on agricultural collectives and state farms; "officials," who performed non-manual labor and probably included teachers, technicians, and health-care workers as well as civil servants and Korean Workers' Party (KWP) cadres; and workers employed in "cooperative industrial units," small-scale enterprises that are attached to larger work units but constitute a very small share of the total. North Korean government statistics showed that the state "worker" category constituted the largest category in 1987 at 57 percent of the labor force. Farmers comprised the second largest category at 25 percent; and officials and industrial cooperative workers, 17 percent and 1 percent, respectively. The occupational structure of

Table 1. Occupation of Sample

Position	N	Percent
Laborer	814	62
Farmer	459	35
Technician	27	2
Soldier	11	1
Communist Party Member	1	–
Government Official	1	–
Total	1313	

the sample appears to roughly mirror the society as a whole (Table 1).[3] Not surprisingly, elites and the military are underrepresented among the refugees although not altogether absent.[4]

Family background is a key determinant of life in North Korea. The regime has conducted a succession of classification exercises, dividing the population into a core class of reliable supporters, the basic masses, and the "impure class." Those lucky enough to be considered as "core" supporters of the government, such as party members or families of war martyrs, are given preferences for educational and employment opportunities, allowed to live in better-off areas, and have greater access to food and other material goods. Those with a "hostile" or disloyal profile, such as relatives of people who collaborated with the Japanese during the Japanese occupation, landowners, or those who went south during the Korean War, are subjected to a number of disadvantages, assigned to the worst schools, jobs and localities, and sometimes winding up in labor camps. In earlier refugee surveys by Robinson et. al. (1999, 2001a, 2001b), conducted in 1999 and 2000, and asking respondents to recall the period from 1995 to 1998, it was found that about 75 percent of refugee respondents were from the "wavering" class and another 8 to 12 percent were hostile; nonetheless, it is interesting that both of the Robinson surveys included "loyal" respondents (17 percent in 1995, 13 percent in 1998), which are estimated to account for 20 to 25 percent of the population as a whole.

By cross-tabulating the occupation of the respondents with the occupation of their parents, we are able to gain some insight into social mobility in Korea (see Appendix Table 1). There is some mobility of workers into the "technical" class, yet the class structure of the society is remarkably stable: more than 90 percent of the refugees surveyed who were laborers also had laborers as parents. Virtually all farmers had farmers as parents. The numbers of farmers or laborers whose parents did not come from one of these two classes is trivial.

Table 2. Education of Sample

Education	N	Percent
Elementary	582	44
High School	696	52
University	16	1
Technical School	15	1
Others	17	1
Total	1326	

The occupational structure is mirrored in predictable ways in the educational background of the sample respondents. After the establishment of North Korea, the government put in place an education system modeled largely on that of the Soviet Union. The lion's share of the respondents is drawn from age cohorts that entered the education system after the introduction of compulsory education, through at least the seventh grade, that was implemented in the late 1950s.[5] The educational attainment of these refugees is shown in Table 2. Most of those interviewed reported having attended middle or high school. A few reported having attended

---

[3] Although a total of 1,346 interviews were conducted, some questions did not elicit responses from each subject or were not accurately recorded. The totals reported in the tables therefore necessarily differ from the total number of subjects, usually by slight margins. Although we do not believe that this problem fundamentally alters the conclusions drawn from the data, it is important to underline that the data was collected under very difficult circumstances and with highly vulnerable subjects. Reported percentages may not sum to 100 due to rounding.

[4] This profile is similar to an earlier, small survey by Lee et al. (2001), who had a somewhat lower percentage for laborers (55 percent), roughly half as many farmers (15 percent) and noticeably more office workers (12 percent).

[5] At the time of North Korea's establishment, two-thirds of school-age children did not attend primary school, and most adults were illiterate. In 1950, primary education became compulsory. By 1958, seven-year compulsory primary and secondary education had been implemented. In 1959, state-financed universal education was introduced in all schools. By 1967, nine years of education became compulsory. In 1975, the compulsory eleven-year-education system, which includes one year of preschool education and ten years of primary and secondary education, was implemented. In the early 1990s, graduation from the compulsory-education system occurred at age sixteen.

technical schools or university. Again, not surprisingly, more highly educated respondents appear underrepresented although not altogether absent.[6]

A final important feature of the sample has to do with place of origin in North Korea (see Figure 1 and Table 3). Relative to the population of North Korea, the northeast border provinces are overrepresented in our sample, particularly North Hamgyŏng.[7] This overweighting does not necessarily present a problem for drawing inferences about the North Korean refugee community, which is also almost certainly dominated by migrants from these areas. However, it suggests caution in interpreting refugee responses as representative of the North Korean population as a whole.

There are two main reasons for this bias, the more obvious being proximity; those living closer to the border have less far to travel. As other surveys have shown, internal travel in North Korea has historically been controlled and exposes the individual to risk, not only of harassment and mistreatment, but imprisonment.

The second reason for the overrepresentation of refugees from the northeast is that these provinces were hit hardest by the famine and food shortages of the 1990s (Smith 2005; Haggard and Noland 2005, 2007); it is important to recount this history briefly.

North Korea has experienced recurrent food shortages throughout its postwar history, but the most devastating of these occurred in the mid-1990s. The North Korean government launched a "let's eat two meals a day" campaign in 1991. In 1992, Public Distribution System (PDS) rations were cut by ten percent, and thereafter distribution became irregular, particularly in the northeast.[8] During 1994, when food shortages started to affect the functioning of the PDS, the North Korean government reportedly stopped sending food shipments to North and South Hamgyŏng and Ryanggang altogether. These provinces included both highly urbanized industrial population centers on the east coast as well as mountainous, traditionally food-deprived areas. These regions have always suffered from food deficits because of the lack of agricultural land and were highly dependent on the PDS system as a result. The famine appears to have started there

Table 3. Original Residence in North Korea

Home	N	Percent
N Hamgyŏng	762	57
S Hamgyŏng	254	19
Chagang	96	7
N P'yŏng'an	83	6
Ryanggang	65	5
Pyongyang	30	2
N Hwanghae	14	1
Kangwon	11	1
S Hwanghae	9	1
S P'yŏng'an	8	1
Others	9	1
Total	1341	

Figure 1. Map of North Korea

---

[6] Again, this is similar to the profile of the Lee et al. (2001) sample, though in that study, nearly 8 percent of the sample reported having attended college, reflecting the higher share of white-collar workers in their sample.

[7] It is worth noting that these provinces have been even more overrepresented in the samples of previous studies (cf. Robinson et al. 1999, 2001; Lee et al. 2001).

[8] After the Korean war, the regime also sent "undesirable" elements of the population to the northeast provinces: prisoners of war, who were potentially affected by the experience; those with religious affiliations; and the politically suspect, as well as criminals.

in 1994, two years before it hit the rice-growing western provinces. The failure of the already poor domestic agricultural production after severe floods in 1995 and 1996, followed by severe drought, resulted in a drastic reduction to food supplies to the PDS. By 1997, the PDS was reportedly only able to supply six percent of the population.

Table 3 shows that more than three-quarters of the refugees came from North and South Hamgyŏng provinces. It is nonetheless interesting that despite its protected status, 30 refugees did come from the capital city of Pyongyang.

Leaving North Korea, Coming to China

The decision to escape North Korea is not a trivial one, particularly given the harsh penalties on both sides of the border. Refugees consider leaving their homeland for diverse reasons, some having to do with inclination ("push" factors), others having to do with information on opportunities in the target country ("pull" factors). But even if there are good reasons to cross the border, the actual act of migration requires resources and planning and is rarely done without some kind of support, be it from friends, family, or experienced traffickers motivated by financial gain, religious conviction, or political fervor. Such networks and connections enable refugees to leave in the first place and provide them with at least some hope of sustaining themselves on the other side of the border.

The Legal Risks

Before turning to the push and pull factors that are generating this flow of refugees, it is important to understand the legal risks North Korean refugees face. Article 12 (2) of the International Covenant on Civil and Political Rights (ICCPR), to which North Korea is a state party, states that "everyone shall be free to leave any country, including his own." There can be little question, however, that North Korean law does not conform to this obligation and that those who "illegally" cross the border or help others to do so face stiff penalties on their return. Historically, unauthorized departure was regarded as an "act of treason" subject to capital punishment. Even with recent changes in the penal code in 2004 that reduced the penalties for border crossing, these laws prohibiting unauthorized departure are in clear breach of the fundamental right to leave one's own country and of conventions to which the North Korean government is a state party.

Prior to changes in the North Korean penal code in 2004, a person who illegally crossed "a frontier of the Republic" faced a sentence of up to three years in a *kwan-li-so* (a political penal labor colony) where conditions are abysmal, torture is practiced, and death rates are high (Hawk 2003). Several factors influenced the severity of the actual punishment meted out to North Koreans who have been forcibly repatriated from China, however. These include the number of times the person had been in China, their background, and whether their movement into China had a political motivation. Those who did not appear politically dangerous were sent to a village unit labor camp, where they spent between three months and three years in forced labor. Women who were suspected of becoming pregnant in China were subject to forced abortions, and in other cases, infanticide was practiced.

Those who are classified as "political offenders" face more severe penalties. The law criminalizes defection and attempted defection, including the attempt to gain entry to a foreign diplomatic facility for the purpose of seeking political asylum. Individuals who cross the border with the purpose of defecting or seeking asylum in a third country are subject to a minimum of five years of "labor correction." In "serious" cases, defectors or asylum seekers are subjected to indefinite terms of imprisonment and forced labor, confiscation of property, or death.

Facilitating exit is also a crime. Under Article 118 of the criminal code, an official with the "frontier administration" who helps "someone to violate a frontier" faces stiff penalties: a sentence in a *kwan-li-so* for a period of between two and seven years.

These risks are compounded because of the stance of the Chinese government, detailed in the accompanying study by Kurlantzick and Mason. North Koreans in China are denied their right to seek and enjoy asylum from persecution. Although China is a party to the Refugee Convention, it is virtually impossible for North Koreans to access refugee-determination procedures through the United Nations High Commissioner for Refugees (UNHCR) or be afforded protection as a group. According to several reports Amnesty International has received from NGOs and contacts in Japan, South Korea, and the United States, China regularly returns North Koreans back to their country of origin without giving them the opportunity to make a claim for asylum, and there are credible reports of torture in the Chinese detention facilities (Amnesty International 2000, 2001, 2004; Lee 2006:53). China sends North Koreans back without making an objective and informed decision that they would be protected against human rights abuses in North Korea. The Chinese government has also arrested and imprisoned NGO activists—most of whom are South Korean or Japanese nationals—and others who have helped North Koreans seeking to leave China and reach South Korea or other final destinations.

Regulations under the 2004 penal code appear to have codified the differential treatment between economic refugees and those cases deemed political. A defector who is sent back to North Korea is subject to interrogation and investigation by the City or County Security Agency. If the Agency concludes that the defector crossed the border for economic reasons, the new code stipulates sentences of up to two years of "labor correction." The government has even signaled the promise of a pardon under the 2004 penal code, and several NGOs operating in the region have confirmed that punishments seem to be less severe than in the past. On the other hand, if the Agency decides that the defector crossed the border for political reasons, he will be charged with the crime of treason. These defectors are still vulnerable to longer-term detention (Kim 2006). Those assisting them have been publicly executed. Changes in the legal code specify relaxed treatment for pregnant women, though in practice these protocols are breached, and in some cases forced abortions continue to be practiced (Lee 2006).

Push Factors

Over the years, the predominant motivation for North Koreans deciding to cross the border into China has fluctuated somewhat. Early interviews with refugees from the famine period and immediately after found, not surprisingly, that hunger and the search for food were a major push factors (Good Friends 1999, 14). By 2002, however, a Human Rights Watch report found that hunger was just one of the motives for flight; others included loss of status, frustration over lack of opportunities, political persecution due to family history, and a desire to live in similar conditions as those North Koreans who live outside of North Korea (Human Rights Watch 2002). Following others who had already left was yet another motive cited by refugees debriefed in South Korea (Lee 2006, Table 1).

The refugees were asked whether they left for economic, political, or other reasons. For the group of refugees interviewed for this study, the economy was the overwhelming reason for leaving North Korea (95 percent); political dissatisfaction and repression were a very distant second (4 percent). In a narrow sense this pattern of responses would appear to confirm the Chinese government's claim that the North Koreans are "economic migrants" rather than refugees fearing persecution (though almost 10 percent of the respondents report having been incarcerated in the labor camps or the political prison system themselves). As we will see in more detail below, economic circumstances in North Korea, as well as the distribution of food, are very closely tied to the political order; as a result, caution should be exercised in interpreting this data.

Pull Factors

How did North Koreans hear about opportunities and conditions in China? North Koreans suffer near total suppression of their rights to freedom of expression, association, and information, and all forms of cultural and media activities are under the tight control of the party.[9] Under these circumstances, little outside information reaches the public. News stories in the official radio and television broadcasts are heavily censored. Testimonies indicate that North Koreans who own radios or television sets are often monitored to ensure that they do not listen to South Korean or Chinese radio broadcasts or see "illegal" foreign television programs. Foreign journalists continue to face severe restrictions of access within North Korea. Foreign journalists who have visited North Korea are accompanied by "official minders" throughout their visits and are not allowed to directly interview ordinary North Korean citizens. They are discouraged from taking their own Korean interpreters; only official interpreters are allowed to accompany them.

Table 4. Sources of Information on China

	N	Percent
Word of Mouth	1,181	89
Media	68	5
Video, Books	12	1
Didn't Know	73	5
Total	1,334	

All these factors have led to lack of credible information for North Korean citizens with respect to China. Under such conditions, it is not surprising that for a vast majority of the refugees "word of mouth" (including rumor and myth) was their primary source of information (Table 4).[10] Remarkably, 5 percent admitted that they had little information on China before going.

The Mechanics of Escape

How, precisely, do people get out of North Korea? Respondents were asked whether they received help getting out of the country, and three-quarters said they did. Of these, slightly more than half reported that they had paid for assistance—suggesting that bribery of officials and/or the emergence of a group of brokers or "coyotes" (Table 5) plays a large role in escape. The presence of corruption and of an underground engaged in such politically risky business suggests broader change in the North Korean economy and that money is playing an increasing role. The second most frequent response for sources of help was "other," presumably family or friends who assisted in the escape. Although it is often thought that missionaries and NGOs are playing a major role in the underground railroad getting out of North Korea, the data reported in Table 5 indicates that in quantitative terms at this stage of the migration process at least, their importance is relatively minor.

Table 5. Sources of Help in Leaving North Korea

Aid from	N	Percent
Money	521	52
Missionary	10	1
NGO	7	1
Other	466	46
Total	1,004	

Post-Migration Plans

An important question is the stability of the North Korean community in China and their intentions with respect to staying, moving to third countries, or going back to North Korea. Nearly one-third of the respondents have been in China for three years or more (Table 6). Here, interpretation of the data is complicated by the fact that the demographics of the migrants (and perhaps their motivations, capacities, and expectations) have changed over time. For most migrants, residence in the Chinese border region where the survey was conducted is not their ultimate goal: it is a temporary residence until they can assemble the resources to continue on to some preferred location for permanent settlement.

---

[9] For overviews of the human rights situation in North Korea, see: Amnesty International (2004), Freedom House (2006); KINU(2006).

[10] According to Lee (2006), some refugees from Pyongyang and Hamhŏng debriefed in South Korea reported watching South Korean television via satellite dishes installed on top of high rise apartment buildings. These cases would appear relatively atypical, however.

Yet while most migrants do not want to reside permanently in China, their "transitional" stay prior to on-migration toward their ultimate destination may be protracted. This pattern is documented in subsequent tables. Refugees who have been in China for a long period may simply have integrated successfully, or they may have dependents such as small children or disabilities that have impeded their on-migration out of the border region. These considerations simply underscore the complexity of the migration process.

Table 6. Length of Time in China

Length	N	Percent	Cumulative Percent
Less than 6 Months	68	5	5
One Year	153	12	17
Two Years	203	15	32
Three Years	475	36	68
More than Three Years	427	32	100
Total	1,326		

Refugees were asked whether they were holding a job, and only 22 percent said that they were. Low levels of employment reported by the refugees may stem from a multiplicity of factors. These would include fear of detection or lack of skills, including language skills. Exploitative work conditions may reinforce such impediments. To be able to work in China, one needs a "*hukou*" (residence permit) or a "*shenfenzheng*" (ID card), which North Koreans, by definition, do not have. The lack of papers places the North Koreans at the mercy of employers willing, for whatever reasons, to employ them illegally. Exploitation, arrest during regular "clean ups" by the police, and denunciation by unhappy neighbors are all common occurrences in this environment.

According to the South Korean Unification Ministry, a secret agreement was signed between China and North Korea in the early 1960s governing security in the border area. In 1986, another bilateral agreement was signed calling for the return of North Koreans and laying out security protocols. These conditions invite the exploitation of the North Korean refugees in China and have pushed them into low-wage "dirty, difficult, and dangerous" work, a common circumstance for refugees (Lankov 2004, Lee 2006). There is some evidence that women on average receive higher wages than men, perhaps due to involvement in the sex industry (Lee 2006, 40).

The survey asked whether the respondent was receiving a fair wage, and only 13 percent said that they were; 78 percent report receiving little wages, and 9 percent report receiving none. (A well-known example of the last case is farm workers who are denied wages after being promised that they would be paid after the harvest.) Admittedly, fairness is a subjective concept. Nevertheless, given that real wages and their purchasing power are unquestionably higher in China than in North Korea, the finding that 7 out of 8 respondents believe that they are being treated unfairly is a strong suggestion of exploitation.

As a result of their tenuous status, a large number of refugees have been dependent on assistance from Chinese nationals. The survey asked whether people received help from Korean-Chinese, missionaries, Chinese, or others. The overwhelming majority (88 percent) report receiving help from the Korean-Chinese community directly, and three-quarters report living with Korean-Chinese (Table 7). Missionaries and mountain hide-outs are the second most frequently cited source of residence. This is striking insofar as missionaries face the most severe punishments and fines because their activity is seen as having a political character. Punishments meted out to missionaries harboring refugees include beatings, long-term sentences, and deportation. Korean-Chinese by contrast are given lighter sentences, and refugees have greater opportunity to simply blend into the community.

Table 7. Current Residence

	N	Valid Percent
Korean-Chinese	984	76
Missionary	68	5
Mountain	68	5
Streets	7	1
Other	166	13
Total	1,293	

It is interesting to note, however, that the share reporting residing with missionaries (5 percent) is multiples of the percentage citing assistance by missionaries in providing help in leaving North Korea. Missionaries play a much larger role in China sheltering refugees after their escape than in assisting with egress. This may simply reflect the greater social "space" for religion in China than in North Korea. Among the "word of mouth" North Korean refugee lore is the advice that once in China one should approach buildings displaying a cross where one will receive assistance.

The government of China maintains that the North Koreans in China are not refugees fearing persecution, but rather "economic migrants." Does this claim stand up to scrutiny? In a narrow sense, desperate economic conditions in North Korea have been the predominant motivation behind leaving. But is this migration intended to be permanent or temporary? Do migrants fear persecution if returned?

On the issue of whether North Koreans living in China intend to permanently return to their homeland, the answer would appear to be a decisive "no": more than 97 percent express no intention of returning to North Korea. And regardless of the situation in China, this opposition to repatriation would appear well-founded: North Korea criminalizes the act of leaving the country, and considers it a political offense even though the motive for leaving may be purely economic or even one of survival. This reluctance to return is particularly striking given the fact that an overwhelming majority of respondents—more than 90 percent—report still having family in North Korea. The North Koreans' well-founded fear of persecution appears to be a fundamental impediment to return, and this simple fact constitutes *prima facie* evidence to support their status as "refugees."

Yet many do go back—at least temporarily, in some cases on multiple occasions. Among our respondents, one-fifth had returned temporarily of their own volition, while more than a quarter of the sample had been repatriated. Of those repatriated, 26 percent (86) had been repatriated twice and another 15 percent (49) had been repatriated three or more times. In these cases, even imprisonment was not a deterrent from trying again upon release. Again, this pattern is consistent with a substantial minority of respondents reporting multiple border crossings in a previous survey (Lee et al. 2001, Table 1).

Table 8. Reasons for Returning to North Korea

	N	Valid Percent
Take Money	172	79
Take Food	24	11
Sell Items/Do Business	11	5
No Hope/Hardship in China	5	2
Others Reasons	5	2
Total	217	

As for their motivations, nine out of ten respondents reported returning to North Korea as couriers bearing food and/or money (Table 8). Comparatively small shares returned to do business or because they found prospects in China bleak.

Table 9. Country of Preference

	N	Valid Percent
South Korea	802	64
USA	238	19
China	179	14
North Korea	13	1
Other	16	1
Total	1,248	

Finally, the survey asked about the preferences of the refugees concerning their ultimate place of domicile; where would they like to live? These answers are reported in Table 9. As can be seen, very few express a preference for living in North Korea. South Korea is the favored destination, followed by the United States. Only one in eight refugees in China stated that it was their preferred final destination. We do not have information on what North Koreans in China previously preferred as country of preference, but it is at least plausible that this low share seeking to remain in China reflects the crackdown on refugees that has occurred over the last five years. If China were to loosen its stance on refugees, China might well become more attractive. As of now, however, the vast majority of refugees would prefer to be elsewhere.

Trafficking of Women

A disturbing finding of our survey is the particular insecurity among women refugees. Following the onset of acute food shortages and the decline of the PDS, women found it increasingly difficult to find daily necessities for their families and many left their homes in search of food or work, including to China. Almost from the moment they cross the border—and sometimes when they are still in North Korea—refugee women are tapped by marriage brokers and pimps involved in human trafficking. Marriage brokers provide North Korean women as wives, particularly in the rural areas where the historical preference for male babies has led over time to an acute shortage of marriage-age Chinese women. Having a Chinese husband, however, does not guarantee a North Korean woman's safety, as she is still subject to repatriation. Moreover, women sold into Chinese families where they suffer physical, sexual, mental, and emotional abuse have very little recourse because of their status. Many women resort to prostitution as a source of income (Human Rights Watch 2002, 12-15; Amnesty International 2004, 28; Muico 2005; Lee 2006). In addition, North Korean women also suffer abuse from Chinese guards along the border and North Korean officials upon repatriation (Faiola 2004).

The survey asked respondents if they knew of women being trafficked in China, and a majority responded affirmatively. Of those respondents, they were asked what the price of a woman secured through a broker would be; the findings are reported in Table 10. The mean reported price of women who are sold was roughly 1,900 RMB (approximately $244), but half were sold for less than 1,700 RMB (roughly $218). Prices vary depending on the age of the woman and whether she is encumbered by dependents, with young, single women fetching the highest prices. These findings are strong testament to both the desperation of refugees and the multiple insecurities they face in the Chinese environment.

Table 10. Reported Price of North Korean Brides in China

	N	Valid Percent	Cumulative Percent
500 to 1,000	164	29	29
1,001 to 1,500	122	21	50
1,501 to 2,000	165	29	79
2,001 to 2,500	20	3	82
2,501 to 3,000	72	13	95
3,001 to 4,000	18	3	98
4,000+	14	2	100

However, growing fears of penalty if forcibly repatriated together with better information on the dire situation of women trafficked in China has begun to attenuate the numbers of North Korean women willing to go to China. Anecdotal reports suggest that the price for women has risen recently (as much as 5,000 to 10,000 RMB for single women in their 20s) in response to dwindling supply (Kato 2006).

Psychological Conditions of Refugees: The Prevalence of Distress

Having left their homes, refugees are often forced to confront isolation, hostility, violence, and racism in their new locations; many suffer from major psychiatric disorders, such as post-traumatic stress disorder (PTSD) as a result of their ordeals, as previously documented by Jeon (2000), Lee et al. (2001), Baubet et al. (2003), and Jeon et al. (2005) among others.[11]

In evaluating the findings, it is helpful to establish some psychological context. First, there is a basic difference between stress and trauma: stress is a normal body response to coping with major life events (such as marriage, births, deaths, or starting or ending a job) or handling routine challenges of daily life such as financial difficulties or traffic jams. Trauma is qualitatively different. Trauma is triggered when a person directly experiences or witnesses such events as unexpected death, including during war or famine, severe physical injury or suffering,

---

[11] Interestingly, the duration of such disorders may actually be lower among refugees than among internally displaced people: individuals who became refugees faced similar traumatic events but usually of shorter duration because they were able to escape (Cardozo 2003). There is no reason to believe that the experiences of North Koreans in China should differ in this regard. However, it is important to note that psychological trauma is a durable and constituted state. Individuals are typically not cured without treatment, as illustrated by the high prevalence of patients with trauma who have been in South Korea for some time.

Witnessing Public Execution (Elementary School 2nd Grade-Age 9)

or physical abuse or assault, including sexual assault. Trauma involves severe and possibly unmanageable stress reactions that can cause a unique kind of physical/emotional shock that escalates the "fight-flight" stress response (feeling angry or scared) into "super-stress" (feeling terrified, stunned, horrified, like your life is passing before your eyes, or so overwhelmed you blank out).

The incidence of traumatic experiences among North Korean refugees appears to be quite high. Nearly 10 percent of the respondents reported having been incarcerated in prison or labor camps. Among these former prisoners, nine out of ten witnessed hunger-related deaths and more than three-quarters witnessed death due to torture. The former prisoners were asked if they had witnessed infanticide within the camps: the killing of babies born to women suspected of having become pregnant while in China and hence delivering mixed-nationality children. This practice had been documented by Hawk (2003) through refugee interviews. Interestingly, only 7 percent of our interviewees responded affirmatively—the vast majority indicated that they had not witnessed this practice.

This pattern of a high rate of affirmative response on general phenomena such as hunger in the prison system and a much lower response on the practice of infanticide suggests that respondents were not simply providing the answers they believed interviewers wanted to hear. This reassurance makes the response to a final question all the more chilling: when asked if they believed that prisoners were used in medical experimentation, a practice alleged by Demick (2004) and Cooper (2005) among others, 60 percent responded that they believed that this did indeed occur.

These findings are broadly consistent with those previously obtained by Lee et al. (2001) for a smaller group of subjects. Majorities of their respondents also reported having personally experienced, witnessed, or heard about the following traumatic events: deprivation with respect to food, water, medical care, and shelter; unnatural deaths or murders of family or friends; brainwashing; forced separations; imprisonment; kidnappings; rape; and abuse. These results obtained for refugees in China are also consistent with the findings obtained for a group of 200 North Korean refugees observed in a clinical setting in South Korea as well (Jeon et al. 2005). For this group, the most frequently reported traumatic event experienced while in North Korea was witnessing a public execution (87 percent), followed by personal experience of a family member, relative, or neighbor dying of starvation (81 percent), witnessing a severe beating (71 percent), witnessing punishment for political misconduct (64 percent), and inability to alleviate a family member's or relative's suffering (61 percent).

Such experiences etch an indelible imprint of horror and helplessness on the body and the mind. The world no longer seems safe, manageable, or enjoyable. People no longer seem trustworthy or dependable. Self-doubt and guilt eat away at self-esteem. Faith and spirituality are shaken or lost.

Trauma can manifest itself in a number of specific behavioral responses. One is a permanent heightening of the natural response of fear and anxiety to a dangerous situation. This happens when victims' views of the world and a sense of safety have changed. Memories of the trauma may provoke fear or anxiety. Other common responses to trauma include increased and/or continuous arousal, manifested in feeling jumpy, being easily startled, having trouble concentrating or sleeping, and impatience and irritability. Such reactions—themselves unusual—may further distress trauma victims as well, particularly if loved ones bear the brunt of this behavior. Sometimes people feel angry because of sustained anxiety.

Grief and depression are also common reactions to trauma. These responses may include feeling down, sad, hopeless, or despairing, and manifest themselves in crying, loss of interest in people or activities, risky behavior

Table 11. Post-Traumatic Stress Disorder Indicators

	Strongly Disagree	Disagree	Somewhat	Agree	Strongly Agree	Total
Feel Anxious	.3%	1.3%	22.8%	46.5%	29.1%	1322
Expect Bad Things to Happen	.2%	.5%	2.3%	63.7%	33.3%	1323
Fear for Family	.1%	.6%	2.0%	62.5%	34.9%	1314
In Fear	.4%	1.8%	14.8%	54.6%	28.4%	1320
Not Able to Do Anything	1.1%	10.7%	31.5%	47.6%	9.1%	1313
Get Angry Easily	1.5%	22.8%	26.9%	34.8%	14.0%	1318
Hard to Concentrate	.5%	13.6%	14.5%	55.0%	16.3%	1312
Hope for the Future	.6%	13.3%	32.9%	49.0%	4.2%	1304
Not Sure of the Future	2.1%	14.6%	39.1%	33.0%	11.3%	1311
Not Able to Reach My Goal	3.1%	10.5%	37.8%	37.4%	11.2%	1319
Current Situation is Hopeless	3.9%	12.9%	41.4%	29.0%	12.8%	1316

associated with extreme discounting of future prospects, and, in the extreme, violent, suicidal, or homicidal thoughts or behavior.

Table 11 shows the results of a range of questions that are typically used to diagnose post-traumatic stress disorder; Table 12 summarizes the mean scores on each question. The survey indicates that a majority of North Korean refugees in China exhibit significant psychological distress as a result of their exposure to traumatic events and the hardships associated with life as a refugee. A majority of respondents show signs of psychological distress that is consistent with PTSD.

Among the questions asked, mean scores are highest for those relating to fear for family and anxiety over their status: "bad things will happen," "always in fear," "usually anxious." Clearly, the sources of this anxiety are multiple and encompass events in North Korea that pushed refugees across the border, the stresses associated with the trip itself, as well as conditions in China once refugees arrived. To get at the immediate causes of stress, however, the refugee respondents were asked about the main reason for their anxiety. Table 13 shows that two-thirds are anxious about being arrested and sent back to North Korea, while another 15 percent identify the related concern over uncertainty about their residence. The second most reported reason for their anxiety is for their family in North Korea (16 percent). Again, these results are echoed by the responses from refugees obtained by Jeon et al. (2005) in a clinical setting in South Korea. The most frequently cited trauma among this sample while in China was "fear of risk to life if discovered while in hiding" (83 percent), anxiety about being in a strange place (81 percent), with family-related concerns also prominent. As we have seen, these reasons for anxiety are warranted.

Table 12. Mean of Psychological Distress

	N	Mean
Usually Anxious	1322	4.03
Bad Things Will Happen to Me	1323	4.29
Fear for Family	1314	4.31
Always in Fear	1320	4.09
Not Able to Do Anything	1313	3.53
Get Easily Angry	1318	3.37
Hard to Concentrate	1312	3.73
Hope for the Future	1304	3.43
Not Sure of the Future	1311	3.37
Not Able to Reach Goals	1319	3.43
Current Situation is Hopeless	1316	3.34

Table 13. Reasons for Anxiety

	N	Percent
Fear of Arrest	826	67
Concern about Family in North Korea	197	16
Concern about Residence	189	15
Hunger	11	1
Other Reasons	4	–
Total	1,227	

Even escape does not bring relief. These findings on the psychological state of the refugee community obtained within China persist among refugees who have made it to South Korea (Baubet et al. 2003, Jeon et al. 2005). Controlled clinical studies by doctors working with North Korean refugees in South Korea found few of their patients to be free of psychological disorders, with rates of PTSD ranging from 30 percent (Jeon et al. 2005) to 48 percent (Baubet et al. 2003).

Attacking a Corn Field (Elementary and Middle School Years)

Yet despite the dangers and difficulties they face in their present situation, the defectors are able to find at least some sources of hope as well as reasons to feel that they are working toward achieving their goals; answers to these questions, while also reflecting adverse circumstances, for most respondents were at least somewhat more positive than those related to anxiety.

Conditions in North Korea

Refugee interviews not only shed light on the plight of the refugees, they also constitute one of the most important sources of information on conditions within North Korea as well. To understand the refugee responses, some background on the recent deterioration in economic conditions is warranted.

Under Soviet tutelage North Korea placed all economic assets under state ownership, abolished markets, and subjected all economic activity down to the minutest detail to central planning. In the 1950s, founding leader Kim Il Sung declared *chuch'e* (*juche*), usually translated as "self-reliance," the national ideology. Ironically, North Korea in fact relied heavily on external support from the Soviet Union and China. Economic conditions began to deteriorate in the late 1980s and the subsequent collapse of the Soviet Union and the Eastern Bloc was a body blow. The economy began to shrink in 1990 and has never fully recovered.

The state was even unable to fulfill its core obligation to feed its people and a famine in the mid-1990s claimed perhaps 3 to 5 percent of the population (600,000 to 1 million people). One response to the famine was an appeal for outside assistance, and by the late 1990s, foreign donors were feeding one-third or more of the North Korean population, primarily through the United Nations World Food Program (WFP). This humanitarian aid program continues to this day, albeit on a smaller scale (Haggard and Noland 2005, 2007).

In response to the shock of the famine, North Korean society spontaneously began to construct a market economy from the ground up, borne out of the coping responses to the trauma of the famine and state failure (Haggard and Noland 2005, 2007). With the state unable to provide, people turned to friends, family, but most importantly, to emerging markets for food and other essential goods. As unemployment swelled, many individuals began to engage in small-scale entrepreneurial behavior, often technically criminal. Such activities included initially barter, and later, monetized transactions with counterparts in China to secure food. These developments have occurred largely in the absence of any well-defined rules, and depended in part on officials "looking the other way" as people did what they needed to do to survive. In 2002, in recognition of these developments, and possibly fearful of their political implications, the state accelerated economic policy changes that in effect decriminalized—but also tried to control—these practices.

The results of this bottom-up marketization and partial reform have been uneven. The resumption of economic growth together with foreign assistance ameliorated outright famine conditions. Some individuals and groups have taken advantage of the new opportunities afforded by the loosening of state control to improve their circumstances. Yet the situation remains dire for some groups. Surveys conducted by the WFP and associated groups document ongoing food shortages and widespread and chronic malnutrition. Conditions among workers in the old state-owned, heavy-industry sector, concentrated in a "rust belt" in the northeast, remain particularly tenuous. Inflation in excess of 100 percent a year continues to be a problem (Haggard and Noland 2007).

In the fall of 2005, the government appeared to reverse the reform trend, at least with respect to the food economy. The government banned private trade in grain, while at the same time threatening to expel the humanitarian-aid groups and negotiating a reduced presence for the WFP. But these developments occurred after the survey was completed.

Table 14. Refugee Views of Conditions in North Korea (percentages)

	Strongly Disagree	Disagree	Somewhat	Agree	Strongly Agree
Kim Jong Il's Government Is Getting Better	43	50	5	2	-
Economy in North Korea Is Improving	40	52	5	2	-
North Korean Government Is Trying to Improve Social Conditions	32	30	17	20	1
Education in North Korea Is Improving	36	29	30	3	1
Restrictions on Citizens Are Tightening	1	7	31	41	21
Can Purchase Goods with Money	1	1	21	74	3
North Koreans Believe South Korea's Economy Is Worse than North Korea's	17	62	3	17	1

What the respondents can address are the conditions and practices existing in North Korea in the wake of the famine and the government's implicit ratification of markets in 2002. Having voted with their feet, it cannot be expected that the refugees would have favorable views of the country. Yet the unanimity about political and economic conditions is striking, as are some particular indicators about the course of economic change (Table 14). The first question, an overall evaluation of the government, might be considered as a kind of approval rating. The results are striking: 93 percent strongly disagreed or disagreed that Kim Jong Il's government was getting better, despite the fact that the worst of the famine had eased at the time of the survey.

The reasons are fairly obvious: most respondents viewed the economy as deteriorating and internal controls increasing: 92 percent strongly disagreed or disagreed that the economy in North Korea was getting better, while 62 percent agreed that surveillance was increasing. Interestingly, assessments of social policy, while negative, were at least somewhat more forgiving than the evaluation of economic or political conditions. This may reflect lingering respect for the package of educational and social benefits built up under communism, and the competency and dedication among many front-line service providers such as doctors and teachers.

Among the most striking bits of information concern the ability to purchase goods with money. Despite negative assessments of the government and overall economy, refugees nearly unanimously provide support for other sources of information that the economy is becoming much more marketized. The marketization of the economy is a double-edged sword, however: while it may contribute to increased efficiency in the aggregate, the impact on individual households could be pernicious, and a wide range of evidence has documented rising inequality within North Korea (Haggard and Noland 2007).

North Korean news coverage has long claimed that conditions in the North are superior to those in the South, despite the fact that per capita income in the South is probably 30 times higher than in the North. Northern news sources also continually accentuate bad news from the South, from short-run economic conditions, to social problems, to the political to and fro that is a feature of any democratic society. According to our survey, such claims are increasingly met with disbelief within North Korea. Refugees were asked whether North Koreans believed that the South Korean economy was worse than North Korea's. Nearly four-fifths of the refugees strongly disagreed or disagreed that they did. One explanation for this finding is that other sources of information are starting to penetrate North Korea, whether through clandestine access to media or from refugees who have returned from China. Another explanation is simply that the limits of credulity are being reached; as a result of the hardships North Koreans have been forced to endure, they have to come to view the claims of their government with increasing skepticism.[12]

---

[12] Another survey of 200 recent defectors found that for 19 percent, foreign radio broadcasts such as Korea Broadcasting System, Radio Liberty, Voice of America, and Radio Free Asia were their main sources of news. Twenty-one percent knew someone who had modified their North Korean fixed-tuner radios to listen to foreign broadcasts, and more than half reported knowing someone who had been punished for listening to unauthorized broadcasts. None reported receiving information through foreign newspapers. There is no way of knowing how representative these defectors are of the general public.

The North Korean Food Economy

A final and particularly revealing set of questions concerned the evolving food economy in North Korea. Everyone in North Korea, with the exception of cooperative farmers, historically depended on the PDS for basic food rations. The PDS in North Korea comprises a very extensive system through which subsidized rations are distributed on a gram-per-day, per person basis, according to occupation. This system has never covered workers on cooperative farms, who depend on their own production. Access to state food supplies—including domestic agricultural production, imports, and aid—is determined by status, with priority given to government and ruling-party officials, important military units, and urban populations, in particular residents of the capital Pyongyang. Before the famine, the PDS reportedly supplied over 700 grams per person, per day to over 60 percent of the population. But the famine resulted in a collapse of domestic food supplies and the PDS could reportedly supply only 6 percent of the population by 1997.

As this system began to break down in the 1990s, people were forced to turn to foraging and the nascent markets for sustenance. Such coping responses have included rearing livestock, growing kitchen gardens and collecting wild foods like edible grasses, acorns, tree bark, and sea algae. In 2003, heightened political tensions with key donor countries and general donor fatigue threatened the flow of desperately needed food aid and fuel aid. Black market prices continued to rise following the increase in official prices and wages in the summer of 2002, leaving some vulnerable groups, such as the elderly and unemployed, less able to buy goods. The regime subsequently relaxed restrictions on farmers' market activities in spring 2003, which led to an expansion of market activity.

Table 15. Primary Food Sources in North Korea

	N	Percent
Government Distribution	37	3
Government Distribution and Individual Effort	217	18
Market	741	62
Other	192	16
Total	1,187	

The survey results indicate that 34 percent of the sample relied primarily on their own individual efforts (18 percent) and other channels (16 percent) for food, which corresponds almost precisely to the share of farmers in the survey (Table 15). If one then interprets the remaining responses as reflecting refugees from urban areas, the survey suggests that only about 5 percent of the non-farm respondents obtained their food primarily through the PDS, while 95 percent got it through the market. Again, these figures roughly correspond to the split between elites and non-elites in the underlying sample. They are also consistent with the results of an earlier study in which only 2 percent of the refugees surveyed reported government rations as their primary source of food (Robinson et al. 2001b, Table 1).

From the standpoint of assessing the overall situation within North Korea—as distinct from the experiences of the refugee community—the overrepresentation of respondents from northern provinces may in this case have affected the results. It is widely believed that the breakdown of the PDS occurred earliest and most completely in these areas (Haggard and Noland 2007). It may be the case that the shift toward the market as the institutional mechanism for allocating food may not have proceeded as far in the country as a whole as the overwhelming pattern of responses in this sample indicates. Nonetheless, the results are striking; the North Korean food economy has clearly become increasingly marketized.

Table 16. Improvement of Food Shortage in the Last Two Years

	N	Percent
Strongly Disagree	451	35
Disagree	415	32
Somewhat	401	30
Agree	37	3
Strongly Agree	11	1
Total	1,315	

Table 16 reports answers to the question of whether the refugees believed that the food situation in North Korea was improving in the recent period. Less than 4 percent strongly agreed or agreed that the food shortage has eased since 2002, although some of the respondents would have left the country before the 2002 policy changes and as a consequence would not have direct personal experience with the post-2002 environment. Nevertheless the pattern of responses establishes an almost universal perception among the refugees that things had not improved in North Korea despite the easing of the worst famine conditions.

Table 17 asks whether North Koreans are voicing their concerns about the food shortages. A shift as fundamental as the one depicted in these responses would have broad political and social repercussions, even in a society as repressive as North Korea. Nine out of ten respondents agreed that North Koreans were voicing their concerns.

A final cluster of questions about the food economy concerns aid. North Korea has been one of the largest recipients of food aid in the world for a number of years. When asked about the aid effort, however, only 57 percent of the refugees knew of the food aid. After a decade of a massive humanitarian effort that at its peak targeted no less than a third of the entire population of the country, more than 40 percent of the refugees did not even know of food aid being sent to North Korea.

Fight with My Brother Over a Bowl of Porridge

The refugees who expressed awareness of the humanitarian aid program were then asked if they themselves had received food aid. Only 3 percent responded affirmatively—more than 96 percent indicated that they had not received aid. These answers do not establish that the respondents did not receive assistance; at its peak, aid was flowing in amounts designed to feed roughly one-third of the entire population of the country. But they do underline the fact that respondents were typically unaware of it.

Table 17. North Koreans Are Voicing Their Concerns about Chronic Food Shortages

	N	Percent
Strongly Disagree	11	1
Disagree	27	2
Somewhat	83	6
Agree	796	60
Strongly Agree	399	30
Total	1,316	

There are a number of possible explanations for this lack of awareness of the foreign-aid effort: It is possible that aid in bulk form was distributed through the PDS and that the refugees received it, but did not know that what they had received was aid. This is the most benign interpretation. It is also possible that the aid was diverted into the market and they purchased it there. In this case they might not have known the source of supply, or if they did, they did not consider it "aid" since they were paying for it. It is also possible that they really did not receive any aid, which would have been channeled through the PDS and other institutional channels, such as hospitals and orphanages.

In assessing the implications of these results, the overrepresentation of northern provinces may again be a factor; we know that these regions were discriminated against in relief efforts. These findings may, therefore, accurately depict the experiences of the refugee community, but may not be representative of the country as a whole.

Finally, when asked who received food aid, 94 percent of the refugees who were aware of the program believed that it went to the military and 28 percent said that it went to government officials; less than 3 percent said that it went to common citizens or others. Again, this does not prove that the aid was diverted to the military and officials. But at a minimum, the responses attest not only to the perceived power and centrality of the military in North Korean life but also to the wider control over information and resources on the part of the regime. In the context of a massive, decade-long multinational humanitarian aid program, North Korean refugees exhibit a significant lack of awareness of the overall aid effort. Their overwhelming impression is that the primary beneficiaries of the aid effort were the military. These findings ought to give significant pause to the humanitarian community.

Conclusion

The North Korean refugee problem has recently become the focus of substantial policy attention in both the United States and South Korea, as the other essays in this study demonstrate. Whatever disagreements there may be over the ultimate resolution of the issue, there should be no disagreement that North Korean refugees in China constitute a highly vulnerable population.[13]

- Refugees face a particular set of vulnerabilities that range from their insecure legal and personal status, risks of deportation, to difficulties in securing livelihoods.

- This survey confirms that refugees—and particularly women—are additionally vulnerable to predatory behavior and trafficking.

- These vulnerabilities have a pronounced effect on the mental health of refugees. An overwhelming number of the refugees struggle with anxiety and fear.

- Finally, refugee assessments of developments in North Korea suggest that the conditions that generated the flow of refugees have by no means disappeared.

Recent developments suggest that the concerns of the respondents in this last regard are fully warranted. A good harvest in 2005 and generous food aid from both South Korea and China allowed Pyongyang to reduce its reliance on multilateral food assistance through the WFP. But the North Korean missile and nuclear tests in 2006 once again put Pyongyang sharply at odds with its neighbors, and is likely to place strong external constraints on the country's economic development and food situation in particular. Japan has drifted toward a full-blown sanctions regime against the country. The United States has exploited its role as a financial center to disrupt North Korea's international financial relationships. China and South Korea have become the country's main economic lifeline, but China is openly disaffected with North Korean defiance, and even South Korea has threatened to withhold further food aid. As in the past, weather conditions have also proven uncooperative; floods in July 2006 once again resulted in crop damage, the full effects of which will not be seen until the spring when shortages typically become acute. The recurrence of more serious food shortages, and even of famine conditions, cannot be ruled out; were these to transpire, a corresponding increase in refugees moving across the border into China can be expected.

Despite their hardships, it is important to recall that the refugees who were interviewed in this study chose to flee North Korea because they believed conditions in China were better than those in North Korea. Few have chosen to go back, and those who do, do so on a temporary basis. Moreover, there is little evidence among this group that they seek to return to North Korea on a permanent basis. Interview accounts of life in North Korea also reveal multiple sources of insecurity, including lack of improvement in either economic or political circumstances, and a food economy that remains insecure for many households. While it is important to focus international attention on the particular plight of the refugee, it is also important to recall that the refugee problem is only the very small tip of a much larger iceberg of repressive conditions within North Korea itself, and remind ourselves that the task of the international community is not simply to improve the lives of North Korean refugees but of all the North Korean people.

---

[13] Although our analysis has focused on the position of refugees in China, preliminary work in Thailand by Chang (2006) suggests at least some of the same problems are visible in that refugee community as well. There are approximately 600 North Korean refugees in Thailand. According to the Immigration Act of Thailand, refugees are considered illegal migrants subject to arrest and deportation. In contrast to China, North Korean refugees do have access to a refugee-status determination process conducted by the UNHCR. However, a number of the refugees have been held in detention centers under poor conditions following their arrest as illegal immigrants or while awaiting final resolution of their cases. The Thai government is also clearly concerned about an increased flow of North Korean refugees. Refugees sheltered by NGOs have been shifted into public detention centers, and public officials have expressed concern about granting North Koreans refugee status. See Chang (2006).

References

Amnesty International. 2000. *Persecuting the Starving: The Plight of North Koreans Fleeing to China.*

Amnesty International. 2001. *Human Rights in China in 2001—A New Step Backwards.*

Amnesty International. 2004. *Starved of Rights: Human Rights and the Food Crisis in the Democratic People's Republic of Korea* <http://web.amnesty.org/library/index/egasa240032004>.

Baubet, Thierry, Marine Buissonnière, Sophie Delaunay, and Pierre Salignon. 2003. "Réfugiés nord-coréens en Corée du Sud. De l'importance d'un « tiers » humanitaire," *L'Autre.* 3:4, 455-69.

Carodozo, Barbara Lopes. 2003. "Mental health, social functioning, and feelings of hatred and revenge of Kosovar Albanians one year after the war in Kosovo." *Journal of Traumatic Stress.* 16:4, August.

Chang, Christine. 2006. "Another Journey to Freedom," report prepared for the Asia-Pacific Human Rights Coalition, Inc.

Cooper, Abraham. 2005. "Toxic Indifference to North Korea," *Washington Post,* March 26.

Demick, Barbara. 2004. "North Korea's Use of Chemical Torture Alleged," *Los Angeles Times.* March 3.

Faiola, Anthony. 2004. "North Korean Women Find Life of Abuse Waiting in China," *Washington Post,* March 3.

Haggard, Stephan, and Marcus Noland. 2005. *Hunger and Human Rights: The Politics of Food in North Korea.* Washington: U.S. Committee for Human Rights in North Korea.

Haggard, Stephan, and Marcus Noland. 2007. *Famine in North Korea: Markets, Aid, and Reform.* New York: Columbia University Press.

Hawk, David. 2003. *The Hidden Gulag: Exposing North Korean's Prison Camps.* Washington: U.S. Committee for Human Rights in North Korea.

Human Rights Watch. 2002. *The Invisible Exodus: North Koreans in the People's Republic of China.* November. <http://www.hrw.org/reports/2002/northkorea/norkor1102.pdf>.

Jeon, Woo Taek. 2000. "Issues and Problems in Adaptation of North Korean Defectors to South Korean Society: An In-depth Interview Study with 32 Defectors," *Yonsei Medical Journal.* 41:3, 362-71.

Jeon, Woo Taek, Chang Hyun Hong, Chang Ho Lee, Dong Kee Kim, Mooyoung Han, and Sung Kil Min. 2005. "Correlation Between Traumatic Events and Posttraumatic Stress Disorder Among North Korean Defectors in South Korea," *Journal of Traumatic Stress.* 18:2, 147-54.

Kato, Hiroshi. 2006. Remarks before meeting hosted by the United States Commission on International Religious Freedom, Washington, D.C., 25 May.

Kim, Soo-Am. 2006. The North Korean Penal Code, Criminal Procedures, and their Actual Applications, Studies Series 06-01. Seoul: Korea Institute for National Unification.

KINU. 2006. *White Paper On Human Rights in North Korea.* Seoul: Korea Institute for National Unification.

Korean Buddhist Sharing Movement. 1999. *Report on Daily Life and Human Rights of North Korean Food Refugees in China.*

Lankov, Andrei. 2004. "North Korean Refugees in Northeast Asia." *Asian Survey* 44:6, 856-873.

Lee, Keumsoon. 2006. "The Border-crossing North Koreans: Current Situations and Future Prospects," *Studies Series* 06-05. Seoul: Korea Institute for National Unification.

Lee, Yunhwan, Myung Ken Lee, Ki Hong Chun, Yeon Kyung Lee, and Soo Jin Yoon. 2001. "Trauma Experience of North Korean Refugees in China," *American Journal of Preventative Medicine.* 20:3 225-9.

Muico, Norma Kang. 2005. *An Absence of Choice: Sexual Exploitation of North Korean Women in China.* London: Anti-Slavery International.

Robinson, W. Courtland, Myung Ken Lee, Kenneth Hill, and Gilbert Burnham. 1999. "Mortality in North Korean Migrant Households: A Retrospective Study." *The Lancet.* Vol. 354: 291-95. July 24.

Robinson, W. Courtland, Myung Ken Lee, Kenneth Hill, and Gilbert Burnham. 2001a. "Famine, Mortality, and Migration: A Study of North Korean Migrants in China," in Holly E. Reed and Charles B. Keely, eds., *Forced Migration and Mortality.* Cambridge: National Academies Press.

Robinson, W. Courtland, Myung Ken Lee, Kenneth Hill, Edbert Hsu, and Gilbert Burnham. 2001b. "Demographic Methods to Assess Food Insecurity: A North Korean Case Study," *Prehospital and Disaster Medicine.* 16:4, 286-92.

Appendix Table 1. Occupational Status of Respondents and Parents

Parents' Status/Position

		Laborer	Farmer	Soldier	Tech	Comm. Party	Admin	Total
Laborer	Count	762	30	4	12	1	3	812
	% within Position or Status in North Korea	93.8%	3.7%	0.5%	1.5%	0.1%	0.4%	100.0%
Farmer	Count	5	450	1	0	0	1	457
	% within Position or Status in North Korea	1.1%	98.5%	0.2%	0.0%	0.0%	0.2%	100.0%
Soldier	Count	4	0	5	0	1	1	11
	% within Position or Status in North Korea	36.4%	0.0%	45.5%	0.0%	9.1%	9.1%	100.0%
Tech	Count	10	1	2	11	1	0	25
	% within Position or Status in North Korea	40.0%	4.0%	8.0%	44.0%	4.0%	0.0%	100.0%
Admin	Count	0	0	0	0	1	0	1
	% within Position or Status in North Korea	0.0%	0.0%	0.0%	0.0%	100.0%	0.0%	100.0%
Total	Count	781	481	12	23	4	5	1,306
	% within Position or Status in North Korea	59.8%	36.8%	0.9%	1.8%	0.3%	0.4%	100.0%

North Korean Refugees: The Chinese Dimension

Joshua Kurlantzick and Jana Mason

China is central to any discussion of North Korean refugees. The vast majority of North Korean refugees exit the country via China, and China remains the permanent or temporary domicile for many. Yet, China's policy toward the refugees is unsettled, the product of changes in the Chinese leadership as well as complex foreign and domestic policy concerns.

In the mid-1990s, when the famine in North Korea was cresting and refugees began to flow in larger numbers, Chinese foreign policy remained insular in a number of respects. The old guard associated with Deng Xiaoping was just passing from the scene, and the aftermath of Tiananmen Square had left the Chinese foreign policy establishment suspicious, resentful, and defensive. In the decade since then, China has developed a more sophisticated, coherent, and internationalist foreign policy. However, the issue of North Korean refugees goes to very basic domestic political issues, ultimately including China's own human rights record. Despite ongoing tensions with North Korea, the two countries continue to enjoy a special relationship. Moreover, China has quite obvious concerns about how political instability or a recurrence of severe economic crisis could spill over into China.

These conflicting foreign policy calculations can be seen more clearly by looking at international refugee law and China's posture toward it. This study begins with a detailed consideration of international obligations under the Refugee Convention, and China's posture and behavior with respect to it. A critical issue of contention is whether the North Koreans are in fact refugees under the Convention, a point that China claims is in dispute; this study outlines in some detail why the North Koreans are in fact refugees under the Refugee Convention. How China's behavior has affected the evolution of U.S. refugee policy under the U.S. North Korea Human Rights Act is then considered before turning briefly to China's obligations under two other international agreements that are also relevant to the plight of North Korean refugees: the Convention against Torture and the Convention on the Elimination of All Forms of Discrimination against Women. The study concludes with some reflections on how and why China might be persuaded to abide fully by its international obligations.

The Refugee Convention

Any discussion of international obligations toward refugees begins—and largely ends—with the 1951 Convention on the Status of Refugees (Refugee Convention 1951) and its 1967 Protocol (which incorporates by reference most of the Convention) (Protocol Relating to the Status of Refugees 1967). Article 1 of the Convention defines a refugee as:

> [Any person who] owing to a well-founded fear of being persecuted for reasons of race, religion, nationality, membership of a particular social group or political opinion, is outside the country of his nationality and is unable or, owing to such fear, is unwilling to avail himself of the protection of that country; or who, not having a nationality and being outside the country of his last habitual residence as a result of such events, is unable or, owing to such fear, is unwilling to return to it.

The rest of the Convention lays out the obligations toward refugees to which parties must adhere. Chief among these obligations, and often referred to as the bedrock principle of international refugee law, is Article 33, the *nonrefoulement* provision, which states:

> No contracting state shall expel or return ("*refouler*") a refugee in any manner whatsoever to the frontiers of territories where his life or freedom would be threatened on account of his race, religion, nationality, membership of a particular social group, or political opinion.

Article 33 is at issue when a country acts to prevent persons who might be refugees from reaching its shores, or when it casts away such persons without first having determined that they are *not* refugees.

The Convention sets out a system for promoting compliance with its provisions. Article 35 of the Convention (and Article II of the Protocol) requires parties to cooperate with the Office of the United Nations High Commissioner for Refugees (UNHCR) "in the exercise of its functions" and to "facilitate [UNHCR's] duty of supervising the application of the provisions of this Convention." UNHCR was established in 1949, two years before the Convention was adopted, by a resolution of the UN General Assembly. The High Commissioner reports annually to the General Assembly through the Economic and Social Council (ECOSOC).

The Convention further provides, in Article 38, that any disputes between parties regarding the interpretation or application of the Convention, which cannot be settled by other means, are to be referred to the International Court of Justice (ICJ). Such referral is to be made at the request of any one of the parties to the dispute. This provision is mirrored in Article IV of the Protocol. However, as noted below, China has made a reservation to this provision and cannot be a party to such referrals—which has had little significance since the ICJ has never heard a case arising under the Refugee Convention.

"Working like a dog and receiving little pay. There's nobody to whom I can appeal." (China)

Notwithstanding the lack of ICJ involvement, there has been no shortage of allegations of non-compliance with the Convention. The subject of most such allegations is the Article 33 prohibition against forced return. This prohibition is so fundamental that UNHCR and many human rights advocates argue that it rises to the level of customary international law, binding even on states that are not parties to the Convention or Protocol. Such a requirement of customary international law presumes that the state in question has not consistently objected to the practice. Even then, however, the practice may be considered *jus cogens*, i.e., so fundamental—like the prohibition against slavery or genocide—that no state is permitted to derogate from it.

In the case of *nonrefoulement*, even states that consistently violate this prohibition do not do so by claiming that they are not bound by it; rather, they claim that the individuals are not refugees or that, for some other reason such as the security-related exceptions in the Convention, the individuals are excluded from refugee protection. The view of Article 33 as customary international law is widely held but not universal. However, there is no argument that parties to the Convention must adhere fully to Article 33 and all other articles to which they have not legitimately noted a reservation.

Articles 1 and 33 together make clear that a state party to the Convention cannot send a refugee back to a place where he or she would likely be persecuted. Implicit in the Convention—the strict Article 33 prohibition read together with the multi-pronged Article 1 refugee definition—is a requirement that states take appropriate steps to *determine* whether an individual is a refugee before sending him or her back to possible persecution. The Convention itself is silent on the type of refugee identification procedures that will suffice.

However, as UNHCR notes, "[I]t is obvious that, to enable states parties to the Convention and to the Protocol to implement their provisions, refugees have to be identified" (UNHCR *Handbook*, para. 189).

Unpacking this obligation—figuring out what it means in practice—has been far from straightforward in the 55 years since the Convention was adopted. Major disagreement has surrounded the questions of who makes refugee determinations, when such determinations are required, and how they are to be made.

The question of who determines refugee status—who decides who is a refugee—is fundamental to the entire system of refugee protection. Because sovereign states are parties to the Convention and undertake obligations regarding the treatment of refugees, the general assumption is that the states themselves will establish procedures to assess refugee claims in accordance with their own legal systems. While UNHCR supervises implementation of the Convention and offers advice to states parties, UNHCR encourages states to develop their own refugee determination systems and, in particular, "advocates that governments adopt a rapid, flexible and liberal process, recognizing how difficult it often is to document persecution" (UNHCR website).

Specific guidance on status determination procedures are found in the UNHCR *Handbook on Procedures and Criteria for Determining Refugee Status* (hereinafter "UNHCR *Handbook*"), which is an authoritative interpretation of the Refugee Convention (that is, it is not binding on states but is persuasive authority and is often cited by domestic courts), as well as in conclusions adopted by the Executive Committee of the High Commissioner's Program (ExCom) during its annual sessions. For example, ExCom has recommended that:

> [A]s in the case of all requests for the determination of refugee status or the grant of asylum, the applicant should be given a complete personal interview by a fully qualified official and, whenever possible, by an official of the authority competent to determine refugee status (UNHCR Executive Committee 1983).

As UNHCR notes, "In countries which are not party to international refugee instruments but who request UNHCR's assistance, the agency may determine a person's refugee status and offer its protection and assistance" (UNHCR website). China, as is discussed below, is a party to the Refugee Convention and yet relies on UNHCR to assess the claims of refugee applicants within China.

Despite the expectations and guidance, state practice on refugee determinations has varied considerably. Most industrialized nations have established their own systems, often within the context of their immigration laws, for adjudicating refugee claims. Many developing countries—some parties to the Convention, like China, and some non-parties, such as Indonesia—have largely left this function up to UNHCR. Yet, neither choice assures consistency in adjudication, either among countries or internally. In the United States, for example, a raging debate has centered on whether the screening protocols for Haitians, Cubans, Chinese, and other asylum seekers interdicted at sea conform to international law. Even the sufficiency of the full-fledged asylum adjudication provided on U.S. territory is frequently questioned, given the numerous factors involved in such determinations. Among the countries that allow UNHCR to assess refugee claims, ensuring UNHCR access to all asylum seekers is far from universal.

China and the Convention

The People's Republic of China became a party to both the Convention and Protocol (through the process of accession) in 1982. China has made two reservations to the Convention, regarding artistic rights and industrial property (Article 14) and access to courts (Article 16). China also has made a reservation to the Protocol's provision regarding the referral of disputes to the International Court of Justice (Article 4), which means that since 1967 China would not have been able to be a party to such referrals.

Since 1958, China has been a member of ExCom. ExCom was established that very year by ECOSOC, as a successor to a UNHCR advisory committee. ExCom originally consisted of 25 member states but now has 70 members, all of whom must be members of the UN or any of its specialized agencies but need not be parties to the Refugee Convention (as evidenced by the fact that China became an ExCom member 24 years before it acceded to the Convention). ExCom members are elected by ECOSOC from among those states with a "demonstrated interest in, and devotion to, the solution of the refugee problem" (UNHCR website). Among its functions, ExCom advises the High Commissioner on policy matters, the use of funds, and "whether it is appropriate for international assistance to be provided through his Office in order to help solve specific refugee problems…" (UNHCR website). ExCom meets annually, but its Standing Committee meets several times a year.

China has not enacted specific legislation to codify its obligations under the Refugee Convention and administers no national refugee adjudication process. However, its 1986 immigration control law permits individuals who "seek asylum for political reasons to reside in China upon approval by the competent authorities" (U.S. Committee for Refugees and Immigrants 2005). For the most part, China has adhered to the typical way that many developing countries carry out its Convention obligations; that is, it allows UNHCR the lead role in refugee determinations. Through its Beijing office (and its Hong Kong sub-office), UNHCR conducts refugee status determinations for the relatively few asylum seekers who arrive there. The UNHCR office in Beijing has a current caseload of approximately 250 refugees and asylum seekers, mostly from Pakistan but also from Somalia, Iran, Afghanistan, and elsewhere. UNHCR provides a small amount of financial assistance to recognized refugees, and China allows them to remain in the country while UNHCR arranges for them to be resettled in other countries. However, the refugees are not permitted to work.

The point to note here is that while China permits non-North Korean asylum seekers of all nationalities to openly approach the UNHCR offices in China and to receive UNHCR refugee status determination and remain in China pending resettlement, North Koreans are explicitly excluded from this process—despite the fact that UNHCR and nongovernmental organizations (NGOs) would gladly assist them, and that South Korea would willingly resettle them (although that willingness could change if the numbers became too large).

China also continues to host some 300,000 individuals from Vietnam who are still technically in refugee status for a number of reasons (a number that makes China look like a rather generous refugee-hosting nation). Most of these refugees—of whom the vast majority are ethnic Chinese—arrived in China in 1979 as a result of the China-Vietnam border war. UNHCR considered all pre-1989 arrivals to be *prima facie* refugees. Nearly all reside in China's southern provinces and are fairly well integrated although many still struggle in poverty. UNHCR provides micro-credits and other assistance to a small percentage of this population.

Neither the UNHCR refugee status determination process nor the provision of UNHCR assistance applies to North Koreans in China. In the late 1990s, when the North Korean famine reached crisis proportions and the number of North Koreans entering China sharply increased, China ended its general tolerance of North Koreans in its territory and started returning large numbers to North Korea. China said at the time, and has maintained since then, that no North Koreans in China are refugees. Rather, China considers them to be economic migrants to whom the Refugee Convention does not apply. China is therefore attempting to simply define the North Koreans out of the Convention. Yet, in the absence of either a national procedure to determine refugee status or cooperation with UNHCR in doing so, China must give the North Koreans the benefit of the doubt and treat them as asylum seekers who are entitled to refugee protection.

As noted in the UNHCR *Handbook*:

> A person is a refugee within the meaning of the 1951 Convention as soon as he fulfills the criteria contained in the definition. This would necessarily occur prior to the time at which his refugee status is formally determined. Recognition of his

refugee status does not therefore make him a refugee but declares him to be one. He does not become a refugee because of recognition, but is recognized because he is a refugee (UNHCR *Handbook*, para. 28).

As successive conclusions and resolutions of both ExCom and the UN General Assembly have made clear, Article 33 applies to both refugees and asylum seekers (UNHCR Executive Committee 1996; 1997a; 1997b; UNGA Resolution 1998). This point is critical to the contention that China is violating the most fundamental obligation of international refugee law.

■ China contravenes the prohibition against the forced return of a refugee each time it returns a North Korean to North Korea against his or her will without taking some action—either on its own or through reliance on UNHCR—to assess whether that person could be a refugee. While China, like all sovereign nations, has the right to regulate immigration, the international obligations toward persons at risk of persecution cannot be negated by immigration control.

As noted earlier, adherence to Article 33 generally requires an individual assessment of each case. In particular, "a *denial* of protection in the absence of a review of individual circumstances would be inconsistent with the prohibition of *refoulement*" (Feller 2003).

Yet, not only does China take no steps of its own to assess refugee status, it does not permit UNHCR access to the China-North Korea border area to assess the status of North Koreans. Beginning in 1997, UNHCR conducted regular fact-finding missions to the border and noted to Chinese officials its concern regarding North Koreans there. During such a mission in May 1999, UNHCR determined that some North Koreans were "persons of concern" (POCS) to UNHCR (UNHCR would have called them refugees if not for certain factors, including the dual nationality issue discussed below). China officially reprimanded UNHCR for this action and has since denied the agency permission to travel to the border. This action is in clear violation of the Refugee Convention, which requires parties to cooperate with UNHCR in its supervision of the application of the Convention. Some advocates argue that UNHCR has failed to sufficiently pressure China since 1999 to reverse this situation. Others doubt that such pressure would be successful and believe that it would further erode relations between UNHCR and China.

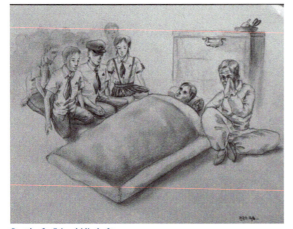

Death of a Friend (died after swallowing almonds)

In August 2002, seven North Korean asylum seekers, aided by activists, attempted to apply for asylum through official channels in China—as is presumed permissible under China's immigration law. This group, which would come to be known as the "MOFA Seven," presented themselves at the gate of the Chinese Ministry of Foreign Affairs (MOFA) and handed to the guards papers that noted their interest in applying for asylum. Members of the group also held up banners that said "We Want Freedom, Help Us" and related messages. Chinese police arrested all seven, and there has been no word since then on their whereabouts. Those involved with their efforts say the seven were almost certainly returned to North Korea and are likely dead.

China's violations of the Refugee Convention go beyond denying UNCHR access to North Koreans in its territory. China has forcibly returned as many as 200 North Koreans a week during certain periods (U.S. Committee for Refugees and Immigrants 2005). The number has fluctuated, with occasional spikes following high-profile incidents, such as when advocates have helped groups of North Koreans enter foreign embassies in Beijing (by rushing the gates, scaling walls, using false papers, etc.). UNHCR has generally avoided becoming publicly involved in or commenting on the response to the embassy incidents (having determined, probably correctly, that it would be counterproductive to its mission in China). Nevertheless, these incidents have attracted much international attention, and China has usually relented by letting the asylum seekers travel on to South Korea. However, China has also responded with other measures: cracking down further at the border; arresting and forcibly returning higher numbers of North Koreans; establishing stricter controls on transportation, particularly into Beijing; and detaining and deporting foreigners who participate in the movement to assist this population and to publicize their plight. In the past year, the number of forced returns has dropped significantly. Because China's tactics have been successful, there are now fewer North Koreans in China to deport.

China has also taken steps to prevent, or at least lessen the likelihood of, future embassy incidents. These include enhancing security in the diplomatic area (with Chinese guards performing military-style exercises in the streets), erecting barbed-wire cordons near embassies, and raiding safe houses where North Koreans have awaited opportunities to enter foreign embassies. In May 2002, China issued a diplomatic memorandum to all embassies and missions in Beijing demanding that foreign governments "inform the Consular Department of the Chinese Ministry of Foreign Affairs in case the illegal intruders were found, and hand over the intruders to the Chinese public security organs" (Human Rights Watch 2002). Subsequently, UNHCR said in a statement that if an embassy hands over a North Korean asylum seeker to Chinese authorities, knowing it will result in forced return, it is tantamount to *refoulement*. The vast majority of governments have ignored China's demands. However, seeking protection by forcing one's way into an embassy compound remains a risky—albeit sometimes successful—endeavor, particularly in the post 9-11 environment. The U.S. state Department's 2004 report to Congress on the situation of human rights in North Korea summarized China's violation of the Refugee Convention as follows:

> China violates Article 31(2) of the Convention by not allowing North Korean asylum seekers in China "a reasonable period and all the necessary facilities to obtain admission into another country." China is also in violation of Article 32, which states that, "Contracting states shall not expel a refugee [who is] lawfully in their territory." China asserts that all North Koreans are illegal economic migrants whom China can summarily return, but it is longstanding and accepted international practice under the Convention and Protocol that persons who assert a need for refugee protection are entitled to a screening by UNHCR or a government to determine whether they qualify for refugee protection. For these same reasons, China also clearly violates Article 33 [*nonrefoulement*]. The mere fact that North Korea has labeled illegal departure from North Korea as an act of treason suggests the importance of evaluating each individual claim before a person is repatriated.

At the UNHCR ExCom meeting in September 2004, the High Commissioner announced that North Koreans in China are "persons of concern." The refugee agency uses this term in various situations, including when UNHCR is not permitted by the host government to conduct refugee status determinations and the individuals are at risk of forced return. In its report to the Standing Committee that March, UNHCR noted that it was "deeply concerned that [North Koreans in China] do not have access to a refugee status determination process and are not protected from refoulement (UNHCR 2004).

Despite its lack of official access to North Korean asylum seekers in China, UNHCR has managed to provide very limited and very quiet protection for a small number of such persons. When it receives confirmation that a North Korean has been arrested by Chinese authorities in Beijing, UNHCR intervenes with the Chinese and argues that the individual should be considered a refugee *sur place* (as discussed below) and allowed to resettle in a third country. A year or two ago, UNHCR was successful in a large percentage of such cases, with China agreeing to allow the individuals to go to South Korea. More recently, however, such efforts have been far less fruitful, possibly due to the heightened political climate surrounding the Six-Party Talks on North Korea's nuclear program.

UNHCR has also had some success in responding to direct requests for assistance (from individuals or non-governmental organizations) even in cases where there has been no arrest. These efforts are conducted with the full awareness of the Chinese government, but UNHCR does not encourage or publicize these efforts for fear not only of jeopardizing the safety of individuals but also of having China withdraw its cooperation should the number of such cases grow too large.

As a result, most North Koreans who have succeeded in leaving China for South Korea have done so by other means: purchasing false identity papers and flying out (Human Rights Watch 2002); boarding boats in Qingdao, Yantai, or other Chinese port cities and sailing to South Korea; or, as discussed above, trying their luck at an embassy or other foreign institution. Other North Koreans use a more indirect route to South Korea or to their destination country, using the "underground railroad" to travel first to Thailand, Vietnam, Mongolia, or elsewhere in Asia. Once there, they submit claims, either directly or through UNHCR, to settle in South Korea (where they have automatic citizenship) or to resettle as refugees in another country. As discussed below, this latter option has recently been used successfully by some North Koreans who have been admitted to the United States as refugees.

China's Bilateral Agreement with North Korea

Since 1986, China and North Korea have been parties to a bilateral agreement (apparently a protocol that followed a 1961 agreement) entitled the "Mutual Cooperation Protocol for the Work of Maintaining National Security and Social Order in the Border Areas" (U.S. state Department 2005). In this agreement, both sides pledge to "cooperate on the work of preventing the illegal border crossing of residents" (Mutual Cooperation Protocol, Article 4). Notwithstanding a history of Chinese famine victims crossing into North Korea in the early 1960s, the main significance of this treaty since its entry into force has been China's agreement to return North Korean "defectors" encountered on Chinese territory. In addition, China's Jilin Province has a local law that requires the return of North Koreans who enter illegally. Both this bilateral agreement and the Jilin law are in clear violation of the UN Refugee Convention. Yet, it is these agreements—rather than the Refugee Convention—that China invokes in justifying its actions toward "illegal" North Koreans.

Binding Arbitration under the Bilateral Agreement between China and UNHCR

Some human rights advocates are calling on UNHCR to invoke the binding arbitration clause of the 1995 bilateral agreement between UNHCR and China (UNHCR-China bilateral agreement 1995). This agreement, which upgraded the UNHCR mission in China to a branch office, requires China to, among other things, provide UNHCR with "unimpeded access to refugees" in China's territory (UNHCR-China bilateral agreement, Article III, para. 5). However, it can be argued that this agreement is not the appropriate mechanism for dealing with China on the North Korean refugee issue.

UNHCR enters into similar bilateral agreements as a matter of course in countries where it has offices; the agency currently has some 160 such agreements in effect. The agreement primarily provides for the diplomatic treatment of the UNHCR office, its staff, and equipment. It is not intended to address substantive issues of the country's treatment of refugees, which are instead governed by the Refugee Convention—at least in countries, like China, that are parties to the Convention.

The "unimpeded access" provision of the agreement also references "the sites of UNHCR projects" (UNHCR-China bilateral agreement, Article III, para. 5) in order that UNHCR can monitor their implementation. This is meant to refer to the UNHCR projects for the nearly 300,000 refugees from Vietnam. Elsewhere, the agreement notes that the UNHCR Branch Office, in addition to fulfilling its functions in accordance with the UNHCR mandate, will "continue to carry out the mandate of the former UNHCR Mission, namely, to assist the Government in the settlement of the Indo-Chinese refugees in the country, and where possible, assist and promote their voluntary repatriation" (UNHCR-China bilateral agreement, Article IV, para. 2). Nowhere does the agreement reference North Korean refugees. Of course, the agreement likewise does not mention asylum seekers from other countries, to which China currently grants UNCHR access, and there is certainly enough room in the agreement, particularly given the references to the UNHCR Statute and mandate, to infer an obligation on China's part to provide access to the North Koreans. The question remains, however, whether pursuing binding arbitration for failure to provide such access is a wise strategy.

A strong possibility exists that the binding arbitration process, if invoked for such purposes, would not be resolved in UNHCR's favor. In fact, if UNCHR were to invoke this clause, doing so could cause China to downgrade UNHCR's presence in China or to expel them from the country altogether.

In addition, calling for arbitration under this bilateral agreement takes the focus off of the much larger issue: China's violation of the Refugee Convention, to which it is a party.

- China's blatant *refoulement* of North Koreans refugees—forcibly returning them to North Korea with no opportunity whatsoever to make a claim to refugee status—contravenes the core obligation enshrined in Article 33, and is as serious a violation of refugee law as can be found.

As noted earlier, the Convention also requires, in Article 35, that parties cooperate with UNHCR. In fact, the bilateral agreement specifically invokes Article 35 of the Convention as a basis for cooperation between the government and UNHCR "in the field of international protection of and humanitarian assistance to refugees" (UNHCR-China bilateral agreement, Article III, para. 1).

Enforcing these Convention obligations through recourse to the International Court of Justice, as provided for in Article 38, would not likely occur for obvious political reasons even if the ICJ were active in such cases and even if China had not made a reservation to the provision concerning the ICJ. Yet, ignoring the Convention and focusing on the bilateral agreement, with the very possible result that UNHCR's operations in China could be significantly hindered (not to mention the chilling effect that could occur in the many other countries where UNHCR works and where such agreements are in force), may not be a realistic alternative strategy.

Ultimately, whatever legal or political mechanism is used to compel China to change its stance toward North Koreans in its territory, it will be up to governments—not UNHCR—to lead the charge. Thus far, China has felt little pressure to effect such a change.

Are These People Refugees?

Most if not all of the North Koreans in China have a *prima facie* claim to refugee status. These claims arise in the first instance because of the persecution through human rights violations that many have already experienced or fear experiencing in North Korea. However, these are not the only grounds for considering the North Koreans as refugees under the Convention. Food is distributed by the North Korean regime based on political loyalty, which means that the famine and subsequent food shortages have had an element of persecution. Moreover, under the North Korean penal code, North Koreans who are returned from China are subject to extremely harsh penalties—in some cases even the death penalty—which means that the North Koreans become refugees "*sur place*" while in China. Each of these grounds for the claim of refugee status deserves elaboration.

Human Rights Violations

North Korea is a highly authoritarian regime with an abysmal human rights record. Even without the famine that wracked North Korea in the mid-1990s (and which was a product, not of natural disaster, but of serious policy errors, as the U.S. Committee for Human Rights in North Korea has noted in "Hunger and Human

Chasing Rats with My Friends During Our Vacation

Rights: The Politics of Famine in North Korea"), it is still likely that many North Koreans who managed to escape the country would have strong claims to refugee status.

In "Acts of Betrayal: The Challenge of Protecting North Koreans in China," Refugees International notes that "[F]ew North Koreans crossing into China have experienced direct, targeted persecution as specified in the Convention definition..." This may be due largely to the demographics of the population that has crossed into China up to this point, or at least at the time of the interviews by Refugees International. Most North Korean refugees in China have been farmers and other rural workers from the far northeast of North Korea. They would be less likely to be involved in political activity than would persons from Pyongyang and other more developed areas of the country.

Nevertheless, the possibility remains that some North Koreans—among those who have already crossed into China or who may do so in the future—may indeed have refugee claims based on one or more of the five grounds specified in the Convention.

Even if they have not experienced such persecution before entering China, they may have a well-founded fear of such persecution if returned, based on one of the five grounds and completely separate from the punishment they may experience for the "crime" of leaving North Korea (discussed below). Because the Convention definition of a refugee is forward-looking, i.e., is based on future fear, the individual would only have to have valid reasons for such fear rather than prove past atrocities, although such past experiences would certainly be persuasive evidence of such fear.

Of the five Convention grounds for refugee status, religion is perhaps the one most discussed by North Korean human rights advocates. In its November 2005 report "Thank You Father Kim Il Sung," the U.S. Commission on International Religious Freedom (USCIRF) presents tormenting accounts of the North Korean government's violations of freedom of religion, thought, and conscience. Among the report's findings are that the government bans religious activity and severely persecutes those caught engaging in such activity, including through summary executions. Although the North Korean constitution formally guarantees freedom of religion and certain religious observances are at times permitted by the government—primarily in an attempt to pacify international bodies such as the UN Human Rights Committee—USCIRF notes that such observances are "highly circumscribed and tightly monitored and controlled" (USCIRF 2005, 13–14). Harsh punishment based on religious intolerance also occurs following the forced return of refugees from China, as is discussed below.

The U.S. state Department's annual human rights reports on North Korea continually note numerous human rights violations committed by the regime of Kim Jong Il. Among the most egregious violations to be documented or alleged are: torture; extrajudicial killings; disappearances; harsh and life-threatening prison conditions; forced abortions and infanticide in prisons; and arbitrary detention. Also widely documented are denials of basic freedoms, government attempts to control all information, and the lack of an independent judiciary (U.S. Department of state 2005a). Numerous human rights organizations have reported on these and other violations. While some violations may apply across the board to all North Koreans, those that are based on political views or other characteristics could constitute persecution and give rise to a Convention-based refugee claim.

Food as a Weapon

The famine, while itself largely a government creation, also created another means by which the government can persecute its opponents. Despite tremendous reliance on international food aid, the North Korean government fails to operate a transparent food distribution system and often denies NGOs access to the country's most vulnerable people—a situation that has led many NGOs to cease operations in North Korea. The government categorizes its population based on perceived loyalty and usefulness to the regime, and channels food aid—and many other entitlements—accordingly.

Thus, food availability and food distribution in North Korea both include a political element. The regime has directed its own food distribution and/or international food aid to individuals and families in the favored political classes. Many North Koreans in China could therefore be regarded as refugees even if they only viewed themselves as coming in search of food, and regardless of the punishment upon return, if they would have reason to believe that such denial of food would continue upon their return.

Refugees International discusses North Korea's practice of withholding food and other assistance from its own people based on political loyalty:

> In North Korea access to public goods — food, education, health care, shelter, employment — cannot be separated from the all-pervasive system of political persecution. Based on an original registration conducted in 1947, the North Korean population is divided into three classes: core, wavering, and hostile, with the latter constituting 27% of the total. There are more than 50 subcategories. The class status of each family is for life and transfers from generation to generation. Members of the hostile class are the last to receive entitlements, which is disastrous when a comprehensive welfare regime such as that established in North Korea collapses, as it did from 1994 onwards. Thus, an entire class of individuals is persecuted through the functioning of North Korea's political system. In this context, there is no meaningful way to separate economic deprivation from political persecution (Refugees International 2005, 13–14).

Refugees International also notes that the North Korean government "further limits access to food and the economic means of survival through a variety of policies that control the lives of North Korean citizens." Such policies include those regulating movement within the country, which hinders the ability to forage for food—an essential means of survival. In addition, government restrictions on the movements and activities of international relief agencies, including the denial of access to certain areas of the country, have a profound impact on access to food for many North Koreans who are viewed by the government as, essentially, expendable (Refugees International 2005, 14).

Punishment for Defection under the North Korean Penal Code

Under North Korean law, defection or attempted defection is a capital crime. The country's criminal code states that a defector who is returned to North Korea will be committed to a "reform institution" for not less than five years. In cases where the person commits an "extremely grave concern," the code provides for the death penalty. North Korean authorities are reportedly most concerned with defectors who, while in China, had contact with South Koreans, Christian missionaries, or foreigners. Numerous sources have noted the brutal conditions at the labor camps to which returned asylum seekers are sent (See, for example, U.S. Department of state 2005b). Based on extensive interviews with North Koreans in China and elsewhere, Refugees International notes that "almost all North Koreans face severe punishment upon deportation, regardless of their original motivation for leaving their country" (Refugees International 2005, 14).

Making Porridge with a Few Noodles

Persons determined to be refugees based on likely punishment if returned home are known as refugees "*sur place.*" The UNHCR *Handbook* states:

> The requirement that a person must be outside his country to be a refugee does not mean that he must necessarily have left that country illegally, or even that he must have left it on account of well-founded fear. He may have decided to ask for recognition of his refugee status after having already been abroad for some time. A person who was not a refugee when he left his country, but who becomes a refugee at a later date, is called a refugee "*sur place*"…A person becomes a refugee "*sur place*" due to circumstances arising in his country or origin during his absence (UNHCR *Handbook*, para. 94–95).

The *Handbook* further notes that an individual's own actions may lead him or her to become a refugee "*sur place.*" Such actions may include political activity in the country of current residence (for example, demonstrations at the embassy of the home country or media interviews that contain political expression), particularly if it is likely that the authorities in the home country would be aware of such activity. Even the act of applying for asylum could in some cases be regarded in this context. Diplomats and other high-profile individuals who "defect" are one example of refugees "*sur place.*"

In the case of the North Koreans, the link is clear. An individual forcibly returned to North Korea from China has obviously attempted to "defect," and such action is a crime harshly punished by North Korean law. Thus, even an individual whose unauthorized departure from North Korea was motivated solely by a search for food—regardless of the link between food and persecution in North Korea—would become a refugee once in China because of the likelihood of harsh punishment upon return.

That nature of the punishment for "defection" is also relevant to this analysis. As the UNHCR *Handbook* notes, "Persecution must be distinguished from punishment for a common law offense. Persons fleeing prosecution or punishment for such an offense are not normally refugees" (UNHCR *Handbook*, para. 56). Even in the case of common law crimes, however, there are situations in which such punishment would be considered persecution under the Refugee Convention. The first such situation is where the punishment is excessive, if the excess is based on one of the five Convention grounds (for example, if persons of a certain race are punished more harshly than members of other races for committing the same crime). Secondly, criminal prosecution for any offense that itself is based on a Convention reason (UNHCR gives the example of "illegal" religious instruction given to a child [UNHCR *Handbook*, para. 57]), or on the basis of a law that violates accepted human rights practices, would itself be considered persecution.

In the U.S. asylum law context, the analysis of "prosecution vs. persecution" often turns on whether the law in question is "fairly administered." For example, punishment—or fear of punishment—solely for bribing a passport official would not qualify the individual for refugee status (even if he used the passport to escape his country) unless the actual punishment was more harsh for this person because of one of the grounds in the refugee definition (AILA Primer, 56–57).

In cases where an individual is subject to legitimate prosecution for a common law crime, it may still be the case that the individual has a well-founded fear of persecution for other reasons. In the case of the North Koreans, the punishment of persons returned from China is both so severe and so closely related to one or more Convention grounds (for example, political opinion, since the "defection" is viewed as treason; religion, since persons who were in contact with Christians while in China are punished more severely; or even race, since returned women who are pregnant are reportedly forced to undergo abortions because the babies are presumed to be Chinese) that it clearly in itself gives rise to a refugee claim, regardless of any additional fears.

The UN Commission on Human Rights passed a 2004 resolution expressing "deep concern" with North Korea's punishment of returnees. The Commission noted that North Korea "treat[s] their departure as treason leading to punishments of internment, torture, inhuman or degrading treatment or the death penalty, and infanticide in prison and labor camps," among other serious human rights violations (Refugees International 2005, 14).

For these reasons, and even without consideration of other persecution that North Koreans may have suffered or may fear, any North Korean who has fled to China should have *prima facie* claim to refugee status based on the likelihood of being persecuted for having exercised the right—recognized in international human rights law—to leave his or her country.

It should also be noted that any or all such persons may have more than one reason for leaving North Korea, including the search for food, and still be considered a refugee as long as at least one such motive relates to fear of persecution based on a Convention ground. Mixed motives may provide for a more complex analysis of refugee status (particularly in the case of North Korea, where such reasons may overlap and may in combination constitute persecution), but it does not disqualify an individual from refugee protection. While recent changes to U.S. asylum law require that a "central motive" for the persecution must be one of the five Convention grounds, the Convention itself places no requirement on the asylum seeker to parse the motives of the persecutor in such a manner. In the above-described case of "food as a weapon," the analysis is even more straightforward. Thus, China cannot avoid its Convention obligations simply by protesting—however loudly—that the North Koreans are "economic migrants."

Dual Nationality

The refugee definition in the 1951 Refugee Convention notes that an individual with more than one nationality must have a well-founded fear of persecution in each country of his or her nationality in order to be considered a refugee in need of international protection.[1] As noted in the UNHCR *Handbook*, this provision is "intended to exclude from refugee status all persons with dual or multiple nationality who can avail themselves of the protection of at least one of the countries of which they are nationals."[2]

The *Handbook* further discusses the requirement that such nationality be "effective" and that, in general, the individual should request such protection and be refused before such protection can be deemed ineffective.[3] While the implementation of this clause has been debated among refugee scholars, it is clear that virtually all North Koreans are able to avail themselves of the protection of South Korea, if they so desire. For this reason, UNHCR officially refers to North Koreans in China and elsewhere as "persons of concern" rather than refugees. This technicality, however, should not in any way diminish the fact that most or all North Koreans outside their country clearly meet the substantive definition of a refugee.

Because the dual nationality clause is included in the U.S. refugee definition as well, a provision to remedy this issue was included in the North Korea Human Rights Act, as discussed below.

---

[1] UN Refugee Convention, Article 1(A)(2)

[2] UNHCR *Handbook*, paragraph 106.

[3] UNHCR *Handbook*, paragraph 107.

One Country's Response:
The U.S. North Korea Human Rights Act

The international dilemma posed by China's violations of its Refugee Convention obligations with respect to North Koreans has been a particular issue for the United States, where active communities of both policy-makers and advocates have taken diverse and sometimes contradictory approaches to remedying the issue. The debate manifested itself in the development and eventual passage in 2004 of the North Korea Human Rights Act (NKHRA). The legislation is broad, addressing humanitarian assistance, human rights, refugees, and other issues. Several observers have noted that some provisions of the legislation reflect a "regime change" agenda toward North Korea while others appear more consistent with an "engagement" approach.

Although earlier versions of the bill had included a large number of refugee and immigration provisions—which were of concern to some refugee advocates because of the potential backlash by China—the final bill included only three that are of significance.

- First, the legislation clarifies that North Koreans should not be barred from eligibility for refugee or asylum status in the United States due to any legal claim they may have to South Korean citizenship.

- Second, it calls on the state Department to facilitate the submission of applications by North Koreans seeking protection as refugees.

- Third, it authorizes up to $20 million for humanitarian assistance for North Koreans outside of North Korea.

The provision clarifying that North Koreans can be eligible for U.S. refugee or asylum status despite their claim to South Korean citizenship was needed to remedy confusion on this issue created by statements of U.S. officials. As discussed above, under both international and U.S. law, dual nationality is a bar to refugee protection unless the individual fears persecution in both countries of nationality, or unless the nationality of the non-persecuting country is found to be "ineffective." At a congressional hearing a few years ago, then-Secretary of state Powell said that the United States could not legally admit North Korean refugees because all North Koreans are entitled to South Korean citizenship under South Korea's constitution. If Powell's interpretation were correct, this would be a barrier to asylum status as well. However, even before the NKHRA, the United States occasionally granted asylum to very small numbers of North Koreans (they were processed through the U.S. asylum system for persons who apply on U.S. territory, rather than being admitted as refugees from overseas). To remedy this problem, Senator Sam Brownback of Kansas, a leading human rights proponent, sponsored legislation that eventually became part of the NKHRA.

The provision requiring the U.S. government to facilitate the submission of applications by North Korean refugees has caused some confusion for the Korean-American population and other advocates of the legislation. Since the vast majority of the North Korean refugees are in China, where neither UNHCR nor refugee resettlement countries have access to them, the large-scale resettlement of North Koreans to the United States is extremely unlikely (although very small numbers have indeed been admitted, as is discussed below). This provision is primarily aimed at circumstances such as when North Koreans seek protection at the U.S. embassy or consulate in China. In such situations in the past, the state Department has responded by saying that the United States does not provide asylum at its embassies overseas. While that statement is technically true (because asylum status is for persons who apply from within the United States), the embassy could simply refer the individual to the U.S. refugee program for potential refugee admission. However, China would have to agree to allow the person to be processed for U.S. admission while still in China, or to leave and be processed elsewhere.

The provision on facilitating refugee applications could also impact the small numbers of North Koreans who escape through the underground network and make their way to Vietnam, Thailand, and other countries and who then seek protection at the UNHCR or a foreign embassy. While most such persons want to go to South Korea, there could be small numbers who have relatives in the United States or who, for whatever reason, would be most appropriately resettled in the United States. The NKHRA also applies to such circumstances, encouraging the United States to resettle at least some of these individuals.

The problem with admitting even small numbers of North Koreans as refugees is that the U.S. has significant security concerns with this population, believing that North Korean spies may seek to enter the country as refugees (a concern shared with South Korea). North Koreans have long been one of three nationalities requiring advance approval from the state Department in Washington before even being referred to the U.S. refugee program (the others being Palestinians and Libyans). Post 9-11 security requirements make it even more difficult for North Korean refugee applicants to be approved.

The NKHRA authorizes $20 million in each of fiscal years 2005 through 2008 to "provide assistance to support organizations or persons that provide humanitarian assistance to North Koreans who are outside North Korea without the permission of the Government of North Korea." Such assistance may include support for refugee camps or temporary settlements, as well as assistance to North Korean women who are victims of trafficking. Thus far, no funds have been appropriated specifically pursuant to the NKHRA, and many observers note that $20 million would be extremely difficult to program, particularly for large-scale efforts. There is no indication that China would allow refugee camps or similar settlements in its territory. Mongolia at one point appeared willing to consider hosting such camps but quickly backed off when news of such talk became public. According to the state Department, other countries hosting North Korean refugees would also oppose direct U.S. assistance to such refugees in their territories. This is not to say, however, that no funding is available for assistance to North Korean refugees. Small amounts of funding from existing humanitarian accounts have for years been made available for limited—even somewhat clandestine—programs to assist North Koreans outside of their country (in one recent funding bill, for example, the Senate recommended $5 million in assistance to refugees in "North Asia"). These programs are not widely publicized because of their sensitivities but have become a critical form of assistance to a discrete percentage of the North Korean refugee population.

The first concrete outcome of the NKHRA occurred in May 2006, when the U.S. government admitted six North Koreans to the United States as refugees. Although a significant development, it was not, as many proponents of the legislation have claimed, made possible solely through the NKHRA. These North Koreans, who were processed in a Southeast Asian country, were admitted through the U.S. refugee admissions program established under the Refugee Act of 1980. The program provides for the overseas processing of refugees, their admission to the United States, and a program of services that includes cash and medical assistance, English language training, job placement, and other services. The United States, therefore, already had the authority and tools needed to admit North Koreans as refugees. What had prevented it from doing so were issues of politics and national security. Through the NKHRA, Congress sent a strong message to the state Department and others within the administration, resulting in the rather historic admission of these six. Since then, the United States has admitted several additional small groups of North Korean refugees.

The Convention against Torture

While most analysis of China's international obligations toward North Koreans appropriately focuses on the Refugee Convention, another potential instrument for the protection of this population is the Convention against Torture and Other Cruel, Inhuman or Degrading Treatment or Punishment (the Convention against Torture or CAT). China signed the CAT in 1986 and ratified it two years later. China made two reservations with respect to the CAT: China does not recognize the competence of the UN Committee against Torture to investigate and respond to allegations of torture in a party's territory (as provided for in Article 20), and China does not consider itself bound by the provision concerning arbitration or referral to the International Court of Justice (paragraph 1 of Article 30).

Article 1 of the CAT defines torture as:

> [A]ny act by which severe pain or suffering, whether physical or mental, is intentionally inflicted on a person for such purposes as obtaining from him or a third person information or a confession, punishing him for an act he or a third person has committed or is suspected of having committed, or for any reason based on discrimination of any kind, when such pain or suffering is inflicted by or at the instigation of or with the consent or acquiescence of a public official or other person acting in an official capacity. It does not include pain or suffering arising only from, inherent in or incidental to lawful sanctions (Convention Against Torture 1984).

Like the Refugee Convention, the Convention against Torture contains a *nonrefoulement* provision. Article 3 of the CAT provides:

> No state party shall expel, return (*refouler*) or extradite a person to another state where there are substantial grounds for believing that he or she would be in danger of being subjected to torture (Convention Against Torture 1984).

Article 3 puts clear responsibility on the host country to assess the potential for such torture:

> For the purpose of determining whether there are such grounds, the competent authorities shall take into account all relevant considerations including, where applicable, the existence in the state concerned of a consistent pattern of gross, flagrant or mass violations of human rights.

Although not nearly as much analysis has been given to China's obligations toward North Koreans based on the CAT as has been done with respect to the Refugee Convention, a straightforward consideration of the two provisions above and of the known facts regarding the post-return punishment of North Koreans appears to make a strong case that China is violating yet another international agreement through its treatment of North Koreans in its territory.

The graphic eyewitness descriptions of atrocities in the labor camps to which returned North Koreans are sent provide evidence of the severe pain and suffering inflicted on the returnees at the hands of North Korean officials. As stated in the penal code itself, the purpose of such treatment is punishment for the act, or attempted act, of defection. To the extent that certain North Koreans—those suspected of being Christian, or women who may be carrying the children of Chinese men—are singled out for even more brutal treatment, discrimination is another clear motive.

As Article 3 of the CAT makes clear, China has an affirmative obligation to seek out information on North Korea's human rights practices. While some sources of such information—such as Human Rights Watch and the U.S. State Department—may be viewed by China as suspect, and while North Korea remains largely a closed society from which reliable information is not easily obtained, there is nevertheless no shortage of documentation on the myriad human rights atrocities perpetuated by the Kim Jong Il regime.

As noted above, the CAT provides that disputes between parties concerning the interpretation or application of the Convention may be submitted to arbitration and, failing that, to the International Court of Justice. However, following a procedure explicitly provided for in the Convention, China has declared that it does not consider itself bound by that provision. Nothing, however, prevents members of the international community from noting and criticizing China's violation of the CAT in its forced return of North Koreans to likely torture.

The Convention on the Elimination of All Forms of Discrimination against Women

Another international treaty of relevance to China's treatment of North Koreans in its territory is the Convention on the Elimination of All Forms of Discrimination against Women (CEDAW). China signed CEDAW in July 1980 and ratified it in November of that year.

Article 6 of CEDAW requires state Parties to "take all appropriate measures, including legislation, to suppress all forms of trafficking in women and exploitation of prostitution of women" (CEDAW 1979). This provision is intended to protect both nationals and non-nationals of the country that is a party to the convention.

The trafficking of North Korean women into China is a significant issue in the border region. Although the numbers are unknown, the vulnerability of women and girls in this situation has been related in first-hand accounts, including those refugees interviewed for this report by Yoonok Chang and her colleagues. According to Refugees International, such trafficking takes primarily two forms:

> One kind is the kidnapping of North Korean women by Chinese or North Korean men along the border who prey on unaccompanied women. The other kind of trafficking is one in which Chinese men pay for North Korean brides and the women willingly marry because they have no recourse but to rely on Chinese men for survival. These partnerships provide a means of hiding from Chinese authorities as well as providing the women with food, shelter, and security (Refugees International 2003).

Human Rights in China (HRIC) notes that while the UN Office of Drugs and Crime has rated China "high" as a destination country for trafficking, the Chinese government has fallen short in efforts to comply with Article 6 of CEDAW. This problem, says HRIC, is due in part to "several deficiencies in information dissemination, legislative definitions, and policy execution" (Human Rights in China 2006).

With respect to North Korean trafficking victims in particular, this failure is no doubt also due to China's overall policy toward North Koreans in its territory—a policy of forced return rather than protection.

While China's failures to comply with Article 6 and any other provisions of CEDAW are not likely to be remedied through arbitration or recourse to the ICJ (the convention provides for such remedies, but China has made a reservation to that provision—and, in any event, this procedure has never been used), international pressure should nonetheless be brought to bear. Some observers have noted that focusing on the full range of vulnerabilities faced by North Koreans in China—as victims of trafficking, victims of torture, children in need of protection, etc.—would broaden both the debate and the range of possible remedies. It could also potentially help by moving the discussion beyond the politically sensitive refugee issue.

Conclusion: The Challenge for Refugee Advocates

That China is violating its international obligations toward North Korean refugees and asylum seekers in its territory is not news to refugee or human rights advocates, to certain policymakers, to China watchers, or to the small percentage of the general public that is aware that thousands of North Koreans are seeking refuge in China. The fiction of a migration driven solely by famine and food shortage becomes more difficult for China to sustain with each new report on North Korea's human rights atrocities. Yet, the North Korean refugee crisis has often—and rightly—been called one of the most significant and yet most "hidden" refugee crises in the world, for the very fact that China has succeeded in preventing what would otherwise be a massive international response in the form of assistance and protection. It would not be hard to imagine hundreds of thousands of North Korean refugees in UNHCR-administered camps in Northeast China, with nongovernmental organizations carrying out their traditional assistance roles while an international resettlement effort—perhaps along the lines of the Vietnamese resettlement model—was underway.

This scenario could occur if China were to stop forcibly returning North Koreans to their home country. Yet, despite the almost certain guarantees of international assistance for the refugees, not to mention the political approval of many key allies including the United States, China continues the forced return of North Koreans for all of the geo-political reasons discussed below. Thus far, China has clearly made the calculation that the international disapproval—which is lukewarm at best—is far outweighed by the benefit of avoiding a mass refugee influx, not angering and/or destabilizing North Korea, and not having to bend on its long-held policy of not interfering in the internal affairs of other countries. Moreover, China's policy avoids the political and security conundrum for South Korea described by Andrei Lankov in his contribution to this report. South Korea, after all, would be the ultimate destination for the vast majority of the refugees.

The question, then, is what—if anything—can be done to convince China to change its policy toward the North Korean refugees? For the moment, refugee advocates are hoping simply to convince China to ease up quietly on the refugees, to cease the arrests and deportations, even while maintaining publicly that nothing has changed. China could save face and maintain its official policy simply by agreeing to give some sort of "humanitarian space" to the beleaguered North Koreans in its territory, even if it must continue to call them economic migrants. Such a change, however nuanced, could have enormous impact for the refugees and would keep open the vital lifeline that is the China-North Korea border. It could also be a first step toward a more formal and comprehensive solution.

However, it is worth considering the prospect that China might in fact take a more forthcoming posture toward its international obligations. While Chinese policy with respect to North Korean refugees remains woefully at variance with international norms and its own professed commitments, there are reasons to believe that long-run trends within China may encourage an evolution of policy in a more constructive direction. China's new foreign policy is visible in its more active mediating role in international disputes, including with respect to North Korea; in its greater interest in multilateral institutions; and in a more active economic diplomacy and pursuit of "soft power." This new course in Chinese foreign policy holds out some hope that China might approach the refugee issue in a more forthcoming way, even if it has not done so to date. Some of these developments are worth reviewing.

Chinese leaders have shown an increasing interest in multilateralism and have advanced cooperative approaches to security. This new approach has been particularly in evidence on the Korean peninsula. Chinese policy has consistently agreed with the United States on the desirability of a non-nuclear Korean peninsula. Following the onset of the North Korean nuclear crisis in October 2002, North Korea insisted on direct negotiations with the United States that Washington refused. Beijing played a crucial mediating role in the spring of 2003 by convening three-party talks that set the stage for a wider multilateral approach through the so-called Six-Party Talks. In July 2006, following the North Korean missile tests, China supported censure of North Korea in the UN Security Council, even if it did not support a tougher resolution drafted by Japan and supported by the United States.

Another crucial element of China's new diplomacy is its rapidly growing economic clout. China employs trade, investment, aid, and the allure of China's economic model to exercise its version of "soft power," particularly with respect to developing countries. In 2005, Chinese trade with North Korea topped $1.5 billion, making China the country's biggest trading partner accounting for some 40 percent of all of North Korea's trade. Between 2003 and 2005, China's outward investment in North Korea rose from roughly $1 million to as much as $90 million. China is building new railway and highway connections through northeastern China to link those provinces to North Korea. With more than 150 Chinese companies now operating in North Korea, thousands of Chinese workers and mid-level managers are residing there, at least temporarily.

Backstopping its investment and its trade is a substantial aid program. China has long assisted North Korea, particularly through implicit subsidies conferred through "friendship prices" on key commodities. China provides food and energy to North Korea, with Chinese fuel shipments—often provided at cost or for free—more than doubling between 1999 and 2005. According to the Korea Trade Investment Promotion Agency, China's grants to North Korea for technical assistance and other aid projects rose from $108 million in 2003 to $145 million the following year. In October 2005, in the wake of an apparent breakthrough in the Six-Party Talks, China upped its promise of aid significantly, suggesting to North Korea that it might provide as much as $2 billion in new assistance.

In addition to direct economic relations and assistance, China is also exporting ideas, emphasizing the benefits of its gradual approach to economic reform. Beijing has worked hard in recent years to sell its economic model to North Korean leader Kim Jong Il. Chinese officials have invited Kim to China for visits to prosperous areas of China like Shanghai, apparently to demonstrate to the North Korean leader that the Communist Party of China has been able to create such prosperity without losing control of the levers of power. In the most recent Kim visit, nine top officials from the Chinese Politburo took him on a route through Shenzhen and Guangzhou that echoed Deng Xiaoping's famous 1992 "Southern Tour," in which Deng promoted continued economic reforms—reforms that helped turn southern China into a region of considerable dynamism. China also reportedly offered scholarships to North Korean students interested in learning more about economic reform, financial systems, and other related topics.

What are the implications of this new foreign policy for the North Korean refugee issue? Because of its desire to project a new international image, some Chinese diplomats, scholars, and opinion leaders are uncomfortable about China's relations with countries like North Korea and Burma. China's willingness to support North Korea is not unlimited: it has gone along with a crackdown on North Korean financial transactions in the Chinese territory of Macau, for example. Yet, China has appeared reluctant to use economic pressure on North Korea as an instrument of diplomacy on the nuclear and missile issues, and is even less likely to do so with respect to human rights or refugee issues. To the contrary, Chinese officials believe that deepening economic relations are more likely to mitigate the refugee problem. China's difference-splitting response in the UN Security Council in July 2006 was typical: it remains unwilling to endorse strong sanctions against North Korea and maintains that its influence over North Korea is limited. Moreover, it has called on the United States to be more forthcoming by making strategic concessions with respect to security guarantees, recognition, and economic aid and has studiously avoided the introduction of issues such as human rights, the Japanese abductees, or the refugee question that might complicate the core negotiations on the nuclear question.

In sum, there are a number of trends in Chinese foreign policy that suggest that it might play an increasingly positive role with respect to North Korea in the future. In the refugee case, however, these general trends rub up against some very sensitive Chinese concerns, and China's willingness to act in a significantly more constructive way vis-à-vis North Korean refugees is by no means assured. As with North Korea itself, the international community must forge a strategy of engagement with China on these issues, appealing not simply to China's stated international obligations but to its changing national interests as well. Stephan Haggard and Marcus Noland take up these issues in the concluding essay of this report.

References

"Agreement between the Government of the People's Republic of China and the Office of the United Nations High Commissioner for Refugees on the Upgrading of the UNHCR Mission in the People's Republic of China to UNHCR Branch Office in the People's Republic of China of 1 December 1995." ("UNHCR-China bilateral agreement").

American Immigration Lawyers Association (AILA). *AILA's Asylum Primer* 4th Ed.

Convention against Torture and Other Cruel, Inhuman or Degrading Treatment or Punishment. December 10, 1984.

Convention on the Elimination of All Forms of Discrimination against Women (CEDAW). December 18, 1979.

Convention Relating to the Status of Refugees. July 28, 1951.

Feller, Erika, Volker Turk, and Frances Nicholson, eds. 2003. *Refugee Protection in International Law: UNHCR's Global Consultations on International Protection.* Cambridge, UK: Cambridge University Press. <www.unhcr.org/cgi-bin/texis/vtx/publ?id=41a1b51c6>

Haggard, Stephan, and Marcus Noland. 2005. *Hunger and Human Rights: The Politics of Famine in North Korea.* Washington: U.S. Committee for Human Rights in North Korea.

Human Rights in China. 2006. "Implementation of the Convention on the Elimination of all forms of Discrimination against Women in the People's Republic of China: A Parallel NGO Report by Human Rights in China." (June).

Human Rights Watch. 2002. *The Invisible Exodus: North Koreans in the People's Republic of China.* (November).

Mutual Cooperation Protocol for the Work of Maintaining National Security and Social Order in the Border Areas (an agreement between the Chinese and North Korean security ministries), Article 4.

Office of the United Nations High Commissioner for Refugees (UNHCR). 1979. *Handbook on Procedures and Criteria for Determining Refugee Status.*

Protocol Relating to the Status of Refugees. January 31, 1967.

Refugees International. 2003. *Trafficking of North Korean Women in China.* (July).

Refugees International. 2005. *Acts of Betrayal: The Challenge of Protecting North Koreans in China.* (April).

UNHCR. 2004. "Bullet point summary of the strategic presentation on UNHCR's operations in Asia and the Pacific," 29th meeting of the Standing Committee," March 9–11.

UNHCR. "Who Decides Who Is a Refugee?" <www.unhcr.org>

UNHCR Executive Committee. 1983. Conclusion No. 30 (XXXIV).

UNHCR Executive Committee. 1996. Conclusions No. 79 (XLVII).

UNHCR Executive Committee. 1997a. Conclusions No. 6 (XXVIII).

UNHCR Executive Committee. 1997b. Conclusions No. 81 (XLVIII).

United Nations General Assembly Resolution 52/103 (February 9, 1998).

U.S. Commission on International Religious Freedom (USCIRF). 2005. *Thank You Father Kim Il Sung: Eyewitness Accounts of Severe Violations of Thought, Conscience, and Religion in North Korea.* (April).

U.S. Committee for Refugees and Immigrants. 2005. "Country Report on China." *World Refugee Survey.*

"Country Report on Human Rights practices, 2004: Democratic People's Republic of Korea," at <http://www.state.gov/g/drl/rls/hrrpt/2004/41646.htm>.

U.S. Department of state. 2005b. "Report mandated by the NKHRA." (February). <wwwc.house.gov/international_relations/109/NKReporttoCongress.pdf>

Bitter Taste of Paradise: North Korean Refugees in South Korea[1]

Andrei Lankov

Discussions of the North Korean refugee problem have quite naturally focused on the difficulties facing those living in China. Yet as Yoonok Chang shows in her paper for this collection, many of these refugees would prefer to live elsewhere, including in South Korea. A small but growing community of North Korean refugees is currently residing in South Korea. Their experience provides insight into the problems of absorbing refugees from a country such as North Korea, with its long isolation from international contact and peculiar social and educational institutions. The problems of absorbing North Korean refugees are not trivial, as both the South Korean government and the public at large are learning.

This chapter considers the history of the North Korean defector community in South Korea, its interaction with South Korean society and changing official and non-official responses to the defectors.[2] In the past, most defectors came from privileged groups in the North Korean population, and their adjustment to the new environment did not pose significant challenges. However, from the mid-1990s onward defectors began to come from the far less privileged groups, and now this community much more closely resembles the composition of the North Korean populace as a whole. If anything, geographically or socially disadvantaged groups are overrepresented among the refugees. Not surprisingly, these refugees face problems in finding and holding work, with education, with crime, and a more general social malaise.

This changing composition of the defector community has not escaped the attention of South Korean officials and analysts, and the political utility of defectors has fallen. Recent years have seen a dramatic but not always openly stated change in the official South Korean attitude toward defectors: from a policy explicitly aimed at encouraging defection, Seoul has moved to the policy of quietly discouraging it. There are two reasons for this new approach. First are the fears that encouraging defection will undermine the policy of peaceful engagement with the North. But the perception is also growing that refugees are outsiders who face insurmountable difficulties in adjusting to the conditions of South Korean society.

This change in perception—from fellow countrymen in need of help to unwanted burden—has important implications not only for the refugees but for South Korean strategy toward the North more generally. Changing views toward refugees help explain in part the broad support for a strategy of political engagement with North Korea.

A History of Defection

According to the South Korean Ministry of Unification, since the end of the Korean War and through the end of 2004, a total of 7,688 North Koreans have defected to the South. This means that as of December 31, 2005, there were about 7,300 defectors living in the South (as of December 2003, 245 defectors had died or moved to other countries, largely to the United States) (Cho 2004). This figure is probably incomplete, since it is reasonable to assume that some defections have not been made public. This is especially likely in the case of former North Korean cadres, army officers, and intelligence and security operatives.

---

[1] This essay is a revised and expanded version of Lankov (2006).

[2] South Koreans commonly refer to all North Koreans now resident in the Republic of Korea as "defectors," using the name applied to high-level communist Korean Workers' Party officials who defected to Seoul in the 1990s.

Although the numbers of defectors have increased dramatically, it is important to keep their number in comparative perspective. Before the Berlin Wall was built, the number of East German defectors averaged 210,000 *per year* between 1949 and 1961 (Cho 2004). The number of East Germans who defected to West Germany over the 27 year-long period from 1962 to1988 added another 562,261 refugees, or an average of some 21,000 annually (Hirschman 1993, 179). Israel – a state with a much smaller population and economy – has accepted between 40,000 and 80,000. Clearly, a full-blown collapse of North Korea could result in a dramatic increase in defections, but to date that possibility appears remote and the overall numbers remain very small.

Table 1. Number of Newly Arrived North Korean Defectors to the South

Before 1970	1970-1979	1980-1989	1990	1991	1992	1993	1994	1995	1996	1997	1998	1999	2000	2001	2002	2003	2004	2005	Total
485	59	63	9	9	8	8	52	41	56	85	71	148	312	583	1,139	1,281	1,894	1,384	7,688

Source: Republic of Korea Ministry of Unification (2002, 2004) and personal communication, Ministry of Unification Settlement Support Division.

Outbound overseas migration has always been viewed with great suspicion by Leninist states. Despite this attitude, however, most of them did allow at least some citizens to move overseas legally, although manifold restrictions and conditions could be imposed on them. North Korea, on the other hand, strictly adheres to the original Stalinist pattern of "zero tolerance" toward overseas migration. Even if the authorities chose to turn a blind eye to the citizens' exit (like the recent large-scale movement to China), the fugitives are nonetheless technically committing a crime.

Nonetheless, the first years of Korea's division were marked by intense cross-border movement as North Koreans fled to the South in large numbers. The estimates for the pre-war period are between 456,000 and 829,000 while estimates from 1950 to 1953 vary between 400,000 and 650,000.[3] Thus, even according to the most conservative estimate, about 900,000 or 10 percent of the entire population fled the North in 1945-1953.

After the end of the Korean War, the number of refugees decreased dramatically. The relative economic strength of North Korea must have been a contributing factor; in the early 1960s, many Japanese Koreans migrated to the North in hope of finding a better life.[4] Still, from the mid-1950s, the North Korean government also maintained an efficient system of border protection. This system was directed both externally (against the possible penetration of South Korean agents), and internally (against any unauthorized attempts to leave North Korea). The demilitarized zone (DMZ) itself is protected by rows of electrified fences and minefields, and any visit to the areas within 40 kilometers of the DMZ requires special permission issued by the central government (which is different from the normal "travel permits" issued by the local police authorities). The beaches in North Korea are also off limits for the commoners, being dotted with landmines and protected by electrified fences. Combined with the presence of patrols and round-the-clock surveillance of the area, escape across the DMZ is truly suicidal.

Until the early 1990s, the number of defectors arriving in South Korea was very small, typically five to ten persons per year. Most of them came from the North Korean elite, since only members of privileged groups had the opportunity to leave North Korea. Among the early defectors were pilots who flew their fighter jets to the South, diplomats who defected while stationed overseas, soldiers of elite units who knew how the DMZ was protected and could outsmart the guards, and fishermen who managed to deceive their supervisors and sailed their boats to the South.

---

[3] The most comprehensive summary of the available estimates, together with a short analysis of how they were arrived at can be found in Foley (2001).

[4] In 1960, the estimated per capita GNP was $172 in the North, compared to $85 in the South. Hamm Taik-young (1999) believes that only in 1974 the per capita GNP of the South finally exceeded that of the North.

These people were welcomed as heroes in Seoul. The South Korean government wanted to attract defectors because of valuable intelligence they brought in as well as because of their propaganda value. Generous benefits were available for those who reached the South, and propaganda campaigns were waged to encourage even more defections.

All defectors were immediately given the full rights of a South Korean citizen. Since the South Korean government has always maintained that it has legal standing as the sole legitimate authority for all Korea, all North Koreans by definition are South Korean citizens. Under the 1962 law, revised in 1978, every defector was eligible for a generous aid package. Apart from this allowance, defectors who delivered especially valuable intelligence or equipment were given additional awards (*porogŭm*). These awards could be very large. For example Yi Ung-p'yŏng, a pilot who defected with his MIG-19 fighter jet in 1983, received an award of 1.2 billion won (*Chosŏn Ilbo* May 24, 1996).[5] This was an astronomical sum, about 480 times the *annual* salary of an average South Korean at the time! Interestingly, prior to 1997 the payments were fixed in gold, not in Korean won, no doubt to reassure defectors who might have had doubts about the stability of paper currency.

Even without these special awards, the payments received by an ordinary defector were quite sufficient to ensure a comfortable life. The state also provided defectors with apartments that became their personal property. Everyone who wished to study was granted the right to enter a university of his or her choice, not a small privilege in South Korea's highly competitive higher education system. For a while after their arrival the defectors were also provided with personal bodyguards who for all practical reasons acted as their personal advisers on matters of daily life.[6] Still, the number of actual defections remained small, due to the combination of factors described above.

After the collapse of the Communist bloc the situation changed dramatically. On the one hand, Communist ideology ceased to be seen as a serious challenge to Seoul, and the ailing North less of a military, political, or ideological challenge. On the other hand, the stream of defectors began to grow just as the political need for them began to diminish. In 1994, the number of defectors suddenly jumped to 52, a figure around which it fluctuated for the next five years before increasing dramatically to over 1,000 a year in the early 2000s. By 2005, the Korean newspapers did not even report ordinary defections any more; only group or elite defections were even newsworthy.

The overwhelming majority of this new wave of refugees passed through China. As Chang shows in her contribution to this report, most of them are not political defectors but rather workers, farmers, and minor clerks from the borderland areas who were driven to China by hunger and destitution.[7] From the early 1990s, those North Koreans who were able to cross the porous Sino-Korean border could find casual employment in the Chinese northeast, and the Chinese police did not initially track them down with the efficiency common under Mao. The radical liberalization of China, combined with the collapse of border control, made possible large-scale defection, and also changed the social structure of defectors in the most radical way.

The South Korean press often writes about the "wave of defectors" or their "exodus," attracting attention to their fast growing numbers. However, the most significant change of the last decade was not so much increase in defectors' numbers, but dramatic transformation of their social composition that began around 1995 and was complete by 2000. In earlier decades, the defectors invariably came from the North Korean elite. Those elite defectors had education, social skills, and adaptability, and could more easily find a place for themselves in South Korean society. Their insider knowledge of North Korean bureaucracy and military was in great

---

[5] According to the *Stat-Korea* database supported by the National Statistical Office <http://www.stat.go.kr>, an average *monthly* wage in 1982 was 209,553 won.

[6] For an overview of earlier legal regulations regarding defectors, see So (1996)

[7] For an overview of the history and current situation of North Korean defectors in China, see Lankov (2004).

demand, and in rare cases when a particular defector had no such knowledge, he could still earn a good income through writing and lecturing.

Nowadays, the situation is different and the composition of defectors is starting to resemble more closely North Korean society as a whole. Out of 4,716 defectors of the period from January 2000 to August 2004, 41 percent were classified by the Ministry of Unification as "workers" (obviously this figure also includes the employees of state-run "agricultural cooperatives"). A further 47 percent are described as "others," largely school students and unemployed housewives. Only 3 percent are described as "professionals", 3 percent as "managers" (including party cadres) and 2 percent as "sportsmen, artists, and entertainers." Of the remaining, 5 percent are made up of "service workers" and 0.7 percent are ex-soldiers (Ministry of Unification, Settlement Support Division). Thus, even by the most generous estimate, well below 10 percent of all recent arrivals belong to the North Korean elite or even to the educated middle classes. The reasons for this changing composition reflect the risks and hardship of transiting through China. Of course, an educated middle class North Korean from Pyongyang might deliberately risk such an ordeal, go to China in order to defect to the South, survive there and probably succeed eventually. However, such a decision comes far less naturally than for those who are driven to China for economic reasons, including food, and who are willing to accept casual work at very low wages.

Another important change in the composition of refugees concerns family and gender. The share of "others" (largely, ex-dependants) in 2000-2004 doubled, increasing from 28 percent to 55 percent. This obviously reflects the increasing frequency of "chain defection"—one defector paving the way for family and friends to follow—of which more will be said below. In 2002, for the first time, the number of women among the defectors also exceeded that of men (55 percent). In 2003, women composed 64 percent of all defectors, and in 2004 their share reached 67 percent (Ministry of Unification, Settlement Support Division). This gender dynamic is reflected in the well-documented fact that women constitute a majority of North Korean refugees in China.[8]

The geographical origin of the recent defectors once again confirms this same trend. Two-thirds (66 percent) of defectors in 1999-2003 are former residents of North Hamgyŏng province, located in the northeastern part of the country; as Chang shows, residents of this part of the country are overrepresented in most studies of refugees in China as well (Kim 2004, 122). It is remarkable that this same province produced a mere 7 percent of all defectors in the pre-1990 period. North Hamgyŏng province has little political clout and has been widely used as a place to settle politically "less reliable" social groups. During the mid-1990s, it was also the region of the country most vulnerable to the famine.

In sum, the typical defector of the early 1990s was a member of the elite: a party cadre or military officer. The typical defector of the early 2000s is an impoverished and undereducated farmer (or, more likely, farmer's family member) from a remote rural area or an under- or unemployed worker.

The Rise of Sunshine

Until the early 1990s, both a succession of South Korean governments and the public at large assumed that the ideal outcome of the North-South conflict would be complete with eventual absorption of the communist North by the capitalist South. Thus, the disintegration of the Communist bloc in the late 1980s was widely welcomed as it seemingly made such a scenario even more likely. However, the anticipated collapse of North Korea did not materialize. It was East Germany that collapsed instead, pretty much in a peaceful manner that had been a dream of policy makers in Seoul. This made lessons of Germany's "unification by absorption" extremely important for the Koreans, although they ultimately proved disappointing.

---

[8] According to a study undertaken in the late 1990s, women constituted 75.5 percent of all North Korean refugees hiding in China at that time (Good Friends 1999). This high figure has been confirmed by other research as well. According to Kwak (2000, 261), women may comprise as much as 80 percent of all refugees.

It is widely believed in South Korea that the current situation in Korea is much less conducive for a successful post-unification development than was the case in Germany. The per capita gross domestic product (GDP) in East Germany was one-third of that in the capitalist West, and some 80 percent of all Germans lived in the capitalist part of the country. In Korea, per capita GDP in the North is one-tenth that in the South, if not less, and South Korea accounts for only 65 percent of the entire population on the peninsula.

The costs of reunification are correspondingly higher. Marcus Noland has argued that "the amount of capital investment needed in the North might be in the order of $600 billion." This seems to be the smallest available estimate, however. Hwang Eui-gak, who, in early 2005, published a new edition of his seminal work on the North Korean economy, estimated the likely "unification cost" at a higher level of $1,200 billion (Noland 2005; *Chosŏn Ilbo*, July 28, 2005). Two specialists on the unification process, Kim Kyu-wan and (Berlin-based) Pak Sŏng-jo, succinctly captured academic pessimism in the title of their book, *North and South: Dead if United* (2005).[9] Tellingly enough, the book's main message did not cause any protest among its numerous reviewers: its authors said what is accepted as increasingly obvious. The South Korean newspapers often remind their readers about the drastic decline of Germany's competitive power and per capita real income after unification.[10] President Roh himself, during his visit to Germany in April 2005, explicitly stated that Germany should be seen as a negative example, to be avoided by Korea (*Korea Times,* April 14, 2005).

Any understanding of Kim Dae Jung's "sunshine policy" must be seen against this backdrop of increasing skepticism about the costs of reunification. The core of Kim Dae Jung's approach was to first create conditions for peaceful coexistence and increased economic and cultural contact. Over time, economic growth and social change would provide the basis for political integration. Kwak Tae-Hwan and Joo Seung-Ho summarize the strategy succinctly: "North Korea's soft landing, or gradual adoption of a market economy and liberal democracy, is desirable and feasible. [...] Economic reforms and an open-door policy, no matter how limited they may be, will set in motion the transformation of the Stalinist regime. As its economic structure begins to change under the impact of market-oriented economic policies and increased contacts with the outside world, its political and social structure is bound to change" (Kwak and Joo 2002, 80).

These changes in political strategy toward the North implied a quite dramatic alteration in both official and public attitudes toward defectors and an increasing ambivalence about refugees. Neither the Kim Dae Jung nor the Roh Moo Hyun governments have wanted to do anything that might jeopardize the stability of its northern neighbour, and this is understandable. The South Korean taxpayer will bear the ultimate burden of North Korea's reconstruction and the manifold economic and social consequences of such a cataclysm.

At the same time, the South Korean government is not willing to reject the old fiction of "one Korea" and officially admit that the North is but another foreign country whose people happen to speak Korean. The South Korean Constitution clearly defines the government in Seoul as the legitimate authority across the entire Korean peninsula. Technically, all inhabitants of North Korea are citizens of the Republic of Korea, and it remains politically impossible to openly challenge this assumption.

This contradiction between a long-standing legal fiction and changed political circumstances means that the more cautious and selective approach to refugees has occurred by stealth and is seldom—if ever—recognized officially. A remarkable incident in October 1999 exemplifies the new course. At that time, the South Korean public was agitated by reports from China where a number of refugees had been arrested and sent back to North Korea. Lim Tong-won, then Minister of Unification, stated to the National Assembly that the "government is ready to accept all North Korean refugees, if they want to emigrate to the South." He also added: "it is the basic principle of the Seoul government to welcome all North Korean refugees, [...] it is in line with the Constitution to accommodate North Korean refugees."

---

[9] The title itself hints at how Koreans translate the famous dictum "United we stand," normally rendered as "Mungch'imyŏn sanda" (literally, "Alive if United")

[10] The articles that cite such data are very common. For example, see *Seoul Sinmun*, November 19, 2002, and *Naeil Sinmun*, July 15, 2005.

Crossing the Tumen River

This statement reiterated the traditional position of the South Korean government that has not changed since 1948. However, the Ministry of Unification immediately "clarified" this ministerial statement. A senior official at the Unification Ministry explained that the minister's remarks refer to a "group of North Koreans who had wrapped up all the necessary procedures for entry into South Korea with the nation's overseas embassies." Such a "clarification" effectively rendered the minister's statement meaningless, since it excluded virtually all of the refugees in China, none of whom have valid passports, and therefore are incapable of "wrap[ping] up all the necessary procedures for entry into South Korea with the nation's overseas embassies."[11] It is remarkable that the *Korea Times* daily, when reporting these developments, simultaneously ran two articles under contradictory headings: one stated "Korea to Accept All NK Refugees" while another said "Seoul Lacks Practical Means to Accept N. Korean Defectors"!

Recently Ch'on Ki-won, a minister involved with helping the North Korean refugees in China, was asked by a journalist to clarify recent ministerial statements: "Is not the [South Korean] government's position to accept all North Korean defectors?" Ch'on replied: "In other words, the government statement means that they will accept those who will have come to them, instead of taking a proactive stance. They merely mean that they will accept those who will be escorted to the embassies in Southeast Asia by the NGO people. But is it not a hard task to get a refugee there?" (*Munhwa Ilbo*, May 8, 2006)

When a refugee manages to contact the South Korean embassy or a consulate in China to enquire whether it is possible to come to the South, he or she is normally denied assistance.[12] In Southeast Asia the situation is different, and at least some individual refugees are assisted by South Korean embassies and consulates. However, even processing their claims usually takes a long time. Without experience and logistical support, crossing China is nearly impossible, especially for refugees who seldom speak Chinese and come from a less-developed society. Thus, in nearly all cases the refugees are delivered there by brokers or NGOs who have developed imaginative ways to avoid the attention of the Chinese police and arrange a border crossing.

Of course, exceptions to this policy exist. High-ranking military personnel, intelligence operatives, and prominent party cadres can expect that the South Korean diplomats will go to great lengths to arrange their trip to the South. The South Korean representatives also try hard to help those former South Korean POWs who were kept in the North after the end of the Korean War (allegedly against their will, even if this might not always be the actual case).[13]

How have these changes in policy affected the actual process through which refugees get to South Korea? Prior to 2000, South Korean missionaries and NGOs played an important role in helping non-elite defectors reach Seoul. Today, the routes for arriving in the South are more varied. Most defectors travel to South Korea

---

[11] Both Lim Tong-won's statement and the "clarification" attracted much attention and were reported by all South Korean media. Here we use the English wording of the *Korea Times*, which reported both the ministerial statement and its effective withdrawal in the same issue, albeit in different articles (*Korea Times*, October 18, 1999).

[12] Stories about would-be defectors who went to South Korean embassies or consulates, but were unconditionally denied assistance, are too numerous to cite. See *Tong'a Chugan* (No. 166, January 1999), *Sisa Chŏrnal* (July 11, 2001), and *Hangyere 21* (March 2, 2004). In the South Korean press one can find virtually hundreds of testimonies about this semi-official stance toward defectors. I have never seen a single report about a defector whose escape was seriously assisted by the China-based South Korean diplomatic staff (unless such a person was a very high-ranking individual).

[13] As of April 2006, there were some 60 former POWs who fled the North (the first such escape took place in 1994) (*Kukmin Ilbo*, April 12, 2006). These escapes are actively supported by the authorities and much discussed in the media. Even though the officially endorsed worldview implies that all North Koreans are South Korean citizens, the plight of the POWs is taken with far greater sympathy, since they are seen as "authentic" South Koreans who found themselves in the North against their will. Few people seem to realize that the POWs found themselves in the North merely a few years after the division of the country, so they are not that different from other North Koreans.

from China with the costly help of professional smugglers or "brokers," usually paid for by relatives in the South or in some other prosperous country.

Predictably enough, defection developed into a business with "brokers" being the key element in the system. Lee Keumsoon writes in a recent report:

> Unlike the risky episodes of the past, border crossing itself is gradually being 'organized' into a kind of systematic profession. There are "senders" inside North Korea and 'receivers' on the Chinese side; some border guards are somewhat passively, and others more actively, involved in the transactions, and all are involved in some form of bribery and secret deals. Most of the professionals have information on South Korea and China through their earlier defection experiences. Based on shrewd preparations and plans, they will help smuggle out family members over a period of many years (Lee 2006, 12).

With very few exceptions, the starting point for a would-be defector is Northeast China. The most common way to arrange a move to South Korea is to escort a defector to Southeast Asia where the local missions normally provide a ticket and travel documents to Seoul. Less common methods include smuggling an aspiring defector aboard a Chinese boat going to the vicinity of Korea or providing him or her with a forged passport and air ticket to Seoul directly from some Chinese city. Once on South Korean soil, the defectors immediately surrender to the authorities who are forced to accept them and provide them with all of the prescribed support. The typical total cost of an average "arranged defection" in 2005-2006 was approximately $3,000 to $4,000, but in cases of a direct air flight from China the fees are likely to be $10,000, since this scenario requires a forged passport.[14]

The $3,000 to $4,000 does not constitute a particularly large sum in South Korea; it is roughly equivalent to two to three average monthly salaries. However, for a refugee hiding in China this amount is far beyond the capacity to pay, since $3 a day is seen as good pay in the refugee community. Nearly the only way to pay these brokers is through defectors or others in the South who are willing to help. This has led to a new and important phenomenon that may be termed "chain defection," which is not very different from the well-known phenomenon of "chain migration." A North Korean somehow manages to get to the South, and after completing the standard procedures receives the first tranche of monetary benefits. This money is then used to smuggle another family member from China. Upon arrival, the newly arrived family member again invests his or her money into bringing yet another member of the same family over, and so the cycle continues until all family members are safely in the South. In 2003, a Korean scholar who has a good knowledge of the refugee community, described the situation in Hanawon, the major training center for newly arrived defectors: "Among its students, there is a not insignificant number of people whose major goal is to get out of the study center as soon as possible, receive their "settlement money" and use this to bring other family members to South Korea." The scholar even lists the preoccupation with such plans as one of the reasons behind the generally poor motivation of the *Hanawon* students (Che 2001).

Although brokers and chain defections are playing the dominant role in the current flow of refugees, another more risky route is to stage a high-profile intrusion into a foreign mission and, once inside, demand safe passage to South Korea. Once the South Korean Foreign Ministry is faced with such a crisis, it has no other choice but to arrange for the refugees' removal to Seoul. However, such an intrusion must be carefully prepared by knowledgeable persons (often including the very same brokers or NGOs); otherwise the "gate-crashing" is likely to lead to the arrest and extradition of its participants, after which the attempted refugees face very serious charges in the North.

---

[14] For a good description of current rates and "business models" used by people's smugglers see *Tong'a Chugan* (No. 292, July 2002) and *Daily NK*, March 31, 2005.

A final option, and perhaps the most common in recent years, is to migrate within China and cross the border from China to a third country whose authorities would then lobby Seoul to accept the refugees. The major countries of choice nowadays are Mongolia and countries of Southeast Asia, Thailand in particular (refugees travel to Thailand by land, via Burma or Laos). As with the "gate-crashing" option, such refugees pose diplomatic dilemmas for the South Korean government, but an open rejection is impossible. A position taken by the Korean diplomatic staff also has some impact on how refugees are treated. The best-known example of this kind of defection involved 468 North Koreans in a "Southeast Asian country," soon known to be Vietnam, in the summer of 2004.[15] The details of this incident are still held secret at the time of this writing, but it seems that Vietnamese authorities demanded that the South Korean government fly the large number of fugitives out of the country, which it had little choice but to do. However, it is known that in the few years that followed that high-profile incident, Vietnamese authorities were on guard and were doing what they could to prevent more North Korean refugees from coming to the country.

The Changing Support System

For the first few decades of intra-Korean rivalry, the South Korean government treated defectors with remarkable largesse. Being a defector from the North was virtually a guarantee of reasonable income and material security, since stipends were life-long, and were accompanied by large lump-sum payments and in-kind benefits such as apartments and access to education. This generosity did not put the state coffers under much strain, since the number of eligible people remained very small.

However, the collapse of the communist systems and the end of the Cold War had a substantial effect on refugee policy, as defectors lost their significance but their numbers increased. In 1993, the laws governing defectors were revised. The new Law No. 4568 (June 1993) and its revised variant Law No. 5259 (July 1997), as well as other newly administrative regulations, marked a radical reduction in benefits available to defectors.

Gone are the times when an ordinary defector could comfortably live off his or her benefits. As of early 2005, defectors are eligible for three kinds of payments following their arrival in South Korea. First, a defector receives *chŏngch'akkŭm* or "settlement money." The amount of this settlement money has been revised a number of times, but these "revisions" have always meant reduced benefits. The last reduction took place in early 2005. Before that change, the total amount of "settlement money" available to the common defector was about $32,000;[16] from January 2005, this sum was fixed at 10 million won (US$9,000) for a single defector (families are paid more, depending on the number of family members). A lump sum of 3 million won is first paid upon arrival while the remaining amount is paid in quarterly installments over the first two years of the defector's new life in the South. An additional 10 million are available to pay for the very high deposits that are typical in Korea when renting an apartment.

Second, to encourage vocational training, refugees are eligible for some additional payments: a monthly scholarship (*changryŏgŭm*) of 200,000 won if they train more than six but fewer than twelve months in an accredited institution of vocational learning, 2 million won payable upon completion of the course, and an additional 2 million won payable upon appointment (Ministry of Unification, Settlement Support Division).

Thirdly, especially valuable defectors are still eligible for special prizes (*porogŭm*), which can be quite significant although those too have gone down in size. For example, Yi Ch'ŏl-su, a North Korean Air Force captain who in 1996 flew his antiquated MIG-19 to Seoul, received an award of 478 million won (at that time this was equivalent to US$600,000) of which 442 million represented his "special prize" (*Munhwa Ilbo*, January 27, 1997, 31). As sizable as this was, it was well below the 1.2 billion won once granted for a similar feat to

---

[15] The mass defection, the largest in Korean history, was widely discussed in the media. See, for example, *Chosŏn Ilbo*, August 4, 2004.

[16] The author expresses his gratitude to the staff of the North Korean Democracy Movement (an association of the North Korean defectors) who provided him with recent regulations, and helped to make sense of this material in a series of interviews in October-November 2004.

another pilot defector—Yi Ung-p'yŏng in 1983. This change no doubt reflects not only the diminishing military value of a MIG-19 fighter jet, but also the diminishing political value of defectors. Former Korean Workers' Party secretary Hwang Chang-yŏp, by far the highest level North Korean defector, was paid the smaller but still significant sum of 250 million won in 1997 (*Munhwa Ilbo,* October 1, 1997, 2). The 250 million won is the largest sum theoretically payable as a special prize under the 1997 law. If managed well and used with reason and moderation, this amount could insure a life-long, lower-middle-class lifestyle, but hardly more. However, these figures are far from typical: even in the mid-1990s, 95 percent of the defectors failed to receive any special prize at all, and high prizes were paid only to a handful of the most important refugees (Kim 1996, 71).

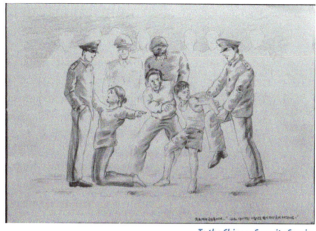

To the Chinese Security Service Officers..."Take us, but please let our son go."

Financial support is only one part of the support system. Immediately after their arrival in the South, defectors are debriefed by South Korean agencies, normally by the National Intelligence Service (formerly the South Korean CIA) and the Ministry of Unification (*Chung'ang Ilbo,* March 19, 2002, 3; *Chung'ang Ilbo,* December 22, 2001, 25). After the debriefing process is over, most defectors go to special classes that are meant to prepare them for their future life in a capitalist society. Since August 1999, such classes are operated by a special educational center located in Ansŏng, a county town some 74 kilometers from Seoul. The center's official name is the "Center for supporting the adaptation of North Korean defectors" or *Pukhan it'al chumin chŏngch'ak chiwon so,* but it is commonly known as *Hanawon.* By the end of 2003, some 3,216 defectors had been admitted to *Hanawon* (Ministry of Unification 2004).[17]

The *Hanawon* program lasts, depending on the situation, between 60 and 75 days. Approximately half of the teaching hours are dedicated to the study of South Korean culture. The remainder is occupied by more practical training: the basics of computer literacy, driving skills for men or cooking for women (the foodstuffs to be found in Seoul shops are largely unknown to the North Koreans). The defectors are also taught some basics of everyday life: how to ride the subway, use a mobile phone, or buy goods at the supermarket. They are also introduced to religious activities (*Hanawon* has a small Protestant church and a Buddhist shrine). The religious education is a "huge success," and a large number of the defectors soon become members of some church, typically Protestant ones (Kim 2005; Sohn 2005). This might be related to the very active role that churches (in particular Protestant churches) have played in supporting North Koreans in China and in facilitating their transfer to the South, as well as the role the churches play in resettlement/integration in South Korea.

Graduates are quite positive about the computer and driving classes.[18] However, within the allocated time it is impossible to equip the defectors with any vocational skills that would facilitate their employment, even for low-level jobs. As most graduates note, the efficiency of this institution, therefore, leaves much to be desired and the South Korean press and even government agencies are highly critical of it. A former graduate of *Hanawon* remarked: "Famous professors delivered some lectures to us, but, frankly speaking, I understood nothing."

After graduation from *Hanawon,* defectors are given the lump sum portion of their "settlement money" and allocated a place of residence. Their first place of residence is determined by the authorities who have recently tried to settle defectors outside Seoul, much to their displeasure. From that time forward, the defector is almost completely on his or her own, and begins to face difficult problems of adjustment to a new life.

---

[17] Defectors over the age of 60 are exempted from training in *Hanawon.*

[18] The South Korean press is almost unanimously critical about *Hanawon* (the only difference is that some blame its administration, while others argue that with such a limited budget the center cannot possibly fare much better). The opinion is shared across the political spectrum — from the leftist *Hangerye Sinmun* to the conservative *Chosŏn chugan.* For the press reports of *Hanawon* and its problems, see *Chosŏn Chugan* (March 1, 2001), *Sin Tong'a* (No. 6, July 2001), *Tong'a Chugan* (No. 263, December 14, 2000), *Hangerye Sinmun* (May 14, 2001). The same critical remarks were confirmed by Pak Sang-hak (2004), the office manager of the North Korean Democracy Movement who himself studied in *Hanawon* in 2000 and by Kim Yun-t'ae (2005) who deals with many defectors.

Problems of Integration

As Cho Yong-gwan points out, "refugees cross the death lines [of the North Korean borders] to come to South Korea, which they have seen as a promised land, but their expectations are not fulfilled here" (2004). Many South Koreans would recall a high-profile incident that occurred in February 1996. At the center of the controversy was a young North Korean named Kim Hyŏng-dŏk who escaped from the North to China in October 1993. After a visit to the South Korean Embassy, whose staff refused to assist the refugee, Kim Hyŏng-dŏk managed to reach Seoul through Vietnam in 1994. His monetary allowance bought him only a tiny apartment in Seoul, a permanent job proved to be almost impossible to find, and dealing with the "locals" was difficult. In February 1996, a disappointed Kim Hyŏng-dŏk together with a friend made another escape attempt, but this time from South to North. During the attempt they were apprehended and jailed, ironically, since an attempt to travel to North Korea without proper permission is still a crime under South Korean law.

In 2001, recollecting his unsuccessful attempt, Kim Hyŏng-dŏk—by that time a university graduate and a clerical worker in the parliament, remarked: "My disappointment was great. First of all, it was difficult to accept an environment in which a person is judged only by his money" (*Hangyere 21*, April 3, 2001). In another interview Kim Hyŏng-dŏk remarked: "I shall not escape again. Utopia does not exist anywhere" (*Kyŏnghyang Sinmun*, April 9, 2001, 29). Alas, this realization sums up the myriad practical difficulties of resettling North Korean refugees, who leave the country with particularly high expectations and limited skills.

There are success stories, of course, but most hail from the elite or come with very particular and marketable skills. Yi Chong-guk, a former cook at *Ch'ŏngryugwan*, the most famous Pyongyang restaurant, has established his own restaurant chain in the South (*Segye Ilbo*, May 12, 2000, 31). Sin Yŏng-hŏi, a former dancer with the prestigious *Mansudae* troupe after her defection became a moderately successful actress (*Segye Ilbo*, March 31, 2000, 16). Her husband Ch'oi Se-ung had for many years worked in the overseas offices of North Korean trade companies, the tell-tale mark of a very high social position (indeed, his father was the head of the Party's financial department). After his defection, Ch'oi founded a company which deals in currency exchange (*Hanguk Ilbo*, February 3, 2001, 7). Even Yŏ Man-ch'ŏl, a former captain in the Ministry of Public Safety (the North Korean police) opened a small restaurant in Seoul, an especially popular choice for many defectors (*Segye Ilbo*, February 18, 2000, 16). However, judging by the rumors in the defector community, even those ventures face serious problems, due to the shortage of management skills among their owners.

Some successful defectors, who once belonged to the North Korean ruling elite, have managed to find employment in research centers. Chang Hae-sŏng, a former North Korean playwright and journalist who at one time specialized in radio dramas about the sufferings of the South Korean people under the American imperialist yoke, currently works in the Institute of Unification Policy and continues his literary and journalistic activities, focusing on North Korea (*Segye Ilbo*, May 2, 2000, 18). His daughter also attracted some attention when she scored a remarkable 380 points in the South Korean version of the scholastic aptitude test, a very unusual achievement for a young North Korean refugee (*Tong'a Ilbo*, December 12, 2000, 30). Many ex-officers continued to serve in the South Korean armed forces, mainly in the intelligence agencies or psychological warfare units. For example, the above-mentioned Yi Ung-p'yŏng who in 1983 fled with his MIG-19 to Seoul, eventually became a colonel and taught at the Air Force academy until his death in May 2002 (*Segye Ilbo*, May 6, 2002, 29).

A majority of the former college students have taken advantage of their right to enter South Korean schools and have found reasonably good work following graduation. In 2001, *Chosŏn wolgan* monthly traced the lives of 11 North Korean students who in 1989-1990 defected from the USSR and other communist countries where they had been studying. Among these students there are two restaurant managers, the owner of a restaurant chain, an LG employee, a writer, a dentist, and two businessmen-cum-programmers who run a successful software company selling mainly into the American market. It is noticeable that a large proportion of this small sample left Korea. Three of the eleven live permanently overseas: two sell cars in the Commonwealth of Independent states (CIS), and one owns a company in Poland. A fourth defector (known personally to the writer) while being technically considered a resident of Korea, in fact resides mainly in the United States where he runs a successful IT business (*Chosŏn Wolgan,* No. 1, 2001). This behavior reflects another widespread trend: the defectors' predisposition toward living and working outside Korea altogether. Apart from defectors who have moved to third countries permanently, there are a number of people who work and live overseas while still technically remaining South Korean citizens, and often employees of Korean companies.[19]

However, it is important to underscore that these success cases are exceptional and constitute only a small minority of the defector community. An increasing body of literature on the North Korean refugees is painting a picture of ongoing problems in adjusting to life in the South.

The typical defector of the early 2000s is a former manual worker or farmer, and is seldom successful in the South. Indeed, most of these defectors live in poverty. According to a 2003 survey of 780 defectors, only 19 percent of them had regular full-time jobs while 42 percent described themselves as "unemployed." In a 2004 survey, the number of "unemployed" defectors was 38 percent. These are very large figures for a country where the unemployment rate fluctuates around 2 to 4 percent (in 2003, it was 4 percent) (National Statistics Office 2006). Moreover these and other studies suggest that those who were employed tended to find work in part-time and casual jobs (Sŏn 2005, 34).

Incomes reflect these difficulties in finding stable, remunerative employment. In 2003, the average monthly income of a defector's family of three was a mere 920 thousand won ($770 at the then current rate) (Yun 2004, 82), while, according to the National Statistics Office, the average monthly income of a South Korean urban family was 2,631 thousand won ($2,200) or nearly three times as much. The national average monthly wage in 2003 was 1,651 thousand won ($1,375) (National Statistics Office 2006). According to a 2003 poll, merely 4 percent of all participants said that they were earning 1,500 thousand won or more. In other words, only 4 percent of defectors earned wages close to the national average or above it (Sŏn 2005, 38).

Getting and keeping a good job is difficult even for those who, strictly speaking, are qualified. The ever-present system of informal connections (alumni connections, known as *hakyŏn* and regional connections, known as *chiyŏn*) normally exclude outsiders, and the defectors are outsiders by definition: with few exceptions, they did not graduate from South Korean universities let alone the good ones that provide a ticket into the elite. As an older defector remarked: "I am not sure whether my son will ever be able to break through the wall of *hakyŏn* and *chiyŏn* and achieve success in Korea" (*Chosŏn Ilbo,* April 16, 2002).[20]

However, it would be an oversimplification to say that the only problem the refugees face is discrimination. The reasons are more fundamental, and have to do with the technological under-development of the North and the corresponding differences in skills and technological cultures. In 2004, the Korean Institute of Labor conducted a survey that indicated clearly the source of refugees' difficulties. The five most common complaints were, in order: "the job does not suit my aptitude" (46 percent of all those who responded to the question), "my future [at this work] is uncertain" (40 percent), "I have no ability to do this work" (37 percent), "problems with discrimination of defectors" (27 percent), and "income is not sufficient" (21 percent) (Sŏn 2005, 49). This range of answers suggests strongly how North Koreans in the South find themselves either in jobs for which they do not have the requisite skills, or lower-skilled jobs that pay inadequate wages.

---

[19] The author remembers how a few years ago he was attending a party with his university friend (once a North Korean student in the then Soviet Union, now a citizen of a West European country) and his wife. The party took place at a Seoul home of one of the defectors, and its participants were largely educated young North Koreans who had moved to the South in the early and mid-1990s. Many participants expressed their envy of the author's friend who was able to live in the West and their wish to find some overseas jobs when/if the circumstances allow. The same tendency of defectors to move overseas is discussed in a large piece published by *Chosŏn Ilbo* (April 16, 2002). The former North Koreans ascribe their decision to discrimination and inability to achieve equality with the "locals" in South Korea.

[20] Complaints about the "glass wall" created by the *hakyŏn-chiyŏn* system are quite common. See *Hangerye Sinmun,* May 22, 2002, and *Munhwa Ilbo,* March 17, 2002.

Another important factor is the defectors' health and their psychological condition. Many of them have serious health problems associated with malnutrition and physical stress they experienced while living in the North, especially in the tragic years of the famine in the mid-1990s. Many of them have been imprisoned and suffered from torture and systematic abuse. Their travel to the South nearly always was very dangerous and stressful, and once in South Korea they find themselves socially disoriented and misplaced. South Korea is, for arriving refugees, an unknown world, which they have difficulty apprehending. They suffer from the loss of relatives and friends, and they often do not understand what their goals and values should be in their new social situation. All these factors adversely influence their ability to adjust to a new life.

They also soon discover that South Korean mainstream public opinion is often indifferent to their plight and does not want to hear much about their grievances. Due to manifold reasons, it is not "trendy" in South Korea to be excessively critical of the North Korean regime, and a majority of younger middle-class South Koreans are skeptical or indifferent to the information about the human rights abuses in the North. Such information is often rejected as "unverifiable" or even as "fakes" created by the right-wing conservative groups. The defectors soon discover that their pain is simply ignored by a majority, and only some Christian activists and/or NGO groups (some rather marginalized in the current South Korean political climate) are willing to listen to them. Not having one's own suffering recognized, being heard with indifference if not with suspicion, is a particularly unbearable form of violence.

The former North Koreans also experience language problems. Generally speaking, the difference between Seoul and Pyongyang dialects is not very large, and they are generally believed to be mutually comprehensible. Nevertheless, in a 2001 poll, a startling 45 percent of defectors stated that initially they were "largely" or "completely" unable to understand South Korean speech while only 24 percent said that they had understood the locals perfectly well (*Segye Ilbo,* January 12, 2002).[21] Apart from differences in word meaning and pronunciation, two important peculiarities of the highly-globalized South Korean society tend to become obstacles for most North Koreans: the wide use of English loanwords and the occasional use of Chinese characters.[22] Both problems become additional obstacles to those defectors who attempt to get white-collar jobs of any kind.

Children of defectors experience problems at school. These problems are especially significant in South Korean society, which places a huge premium on a good education and a university degree. Low grades at high school virtually ensure that a person will be confined to a badly paid manual job for the rest of his or her life.

Volunteers who work with defector children say: "Initially [they] understand no more than 50 percent of a lesson, and the structure of tests and the content of textbooks are unusual to them. Thus the first lessons cause great disappointment. Their difficulties are aggravated by the fact that during their trip [to the South] they have missed one to three years of study and cannot study together with their peers but had to attend classes with younger children instead" (*Chosŏn Chugan,* June 28, 2001). Kŭm Myŏng-ja who runs the largest counseling project for the children of defectors, admitted in her interview with the present author that the problems, especially for boys, are quite pronounced. She underlined that there is a clear correlation between family status in North Korea and academic success of children in the South; children of better-educated families, largely from Pyongyang and other large cities, tend to adjust better (Kŭm 2005). During a survey of defectors' children in 1999, 34 percent described their relations with schoolmates as "bad" (*Segye Ilbo,* June 30, 2000, 16). A large number of teenage defectors are subjected to bullying at their schools (*Sisa Chŏrnal,* July 25, 2002). It is no surprise that

---

[21] The research was ordered by the Ministry of Culture and Tourism, and conducted by the scholars from Konyang University.

[22] The statements and complaints about difficulties with English and Chinese characters have become commonplace in interviews with defectors. I cite just a few of the many relevant examples: a defector complains that he is unable to read even signboards and ads (*Munhwa Ilbo,* January 21, 1997, 5); a defector says he cannot read even a name on a name card—names are normally written in Chinese characters (*Hanguk Ilbo,* February 20, 1997, 5); a defector states that problems with English loanwords and Chinese characters are the major obstacle in his adjustment to a new life (*Segye Ilbo,* October 22, 1995, 22); and a high school student says that he often does not understand his classmates who use many "foreign words" (*Sisa Chŏrnal* July 25, 2002). In the above mentioned study, 76 percent complained about their inability to understand English and 70 percent, Chinese characters (*Segye Ilbo,* January 12, 2002, 8).

many try to hide their North Korean origin and lie to their classmates that they "used to live in China" (*Sisa Chŏrnal,* July 25, 2002).

A dangerous trend over recent years is the increasing involvement of the refugees in criminal activity. In 1996, the Korean press widely reported the defection of Chŏng Sun-yŏng, a distant relative of Chŏng Chu-yŏng, the founding father of the Hyundai Group. She arrived in the South with her two children. At the time, this escape made headlines–partially because escapes by families were still rare in the mid-1990s, and partially because the country's most powerful tycoon was actively and personally involved in the event. Chŏng Chu-yŏng bought his relatives a good house and helped Chŏng Chu-yŏng secure a stable job. Nevertheless, in 2000 this story had an unexpected epilogue: both Chŏng and her elder son found themselves in jail. The son was convicted of theft and pimping, while the mother was jailed for fraud (*Segye Ilbo,* June 30, 2000).

In 2002 alone, the defectors committed 89 crimes, or 28 crimes per 1,000 defectors. Since the average crime level in Korea was 17 per 1,000, this indicates that the crime rate among the defectors was 2 times higher than the South Korean average (*Tonga Ilbo,* October 4, 2004, 8).

This picture of defectors might appear quite grim, and is indeed seen by many South Koreans with great unease; some articles about and interviews with defectors are so critical that they are reprinted in North Korea for use as propaganda material.[23] However, one must be careful about the precise nature of the problem. There can be little question that most North Koreans are materially better off in South Korea than they were in the North. This is often true even in regard to former members of privileged North Korean groups. One such top-level defector, Cho Sŏng-gun, told a South Korean journalist: "Had I been a son of Kim Il Sung, I do not know whether I would defect to South Korea. However, among those below this level, even a North Korean minister or deputy minister, live worse than ordinary South Koreans" (*Chosŏn Wolgan*, No. 1, 2001). This same sentiment was expressed to the author by another defector (Pak 2004): "Many people say that the material life here is ten times better than in the North. Well, maybe it is a hundred times better!"

However, these material benefits are offset to some extent by relative income disparities, inequality, and alienation between the refugees and the host community. In addition to the material differences associated with their lower-class status in South Korea, former North Koreans quickly find out that the attitudes and values of South Korean society pose barriers as well. A South Korean leftist journalist writes: "North Koreans, not used to capitalism, are surprised with the individualistic style of relations between people in the South" (*Hangyerye Sinmun,* August 23, 2000, 3). One of the most prosperous defectors, the owner of a restaurant chain, Chŏng Chŏl-u, noted: "North Korea is poor. But its people are close to each other. It has nothing like the local (South Korean) heartlessness […] This is a society where everything is decided by money" (*Tonga Ilbo,* January 24, 1999, 5). The remarks about alienation felt by defectors can be found in all publications on this topic.[24]

It is important to note that there are signs of dissatisfaction and alienation on the other side as well. The South Koreans who regularly interact with defectors are few in number and seldom vent their frustrations openly, but the anecdotal evidence suggests that South Koreans often look at defectors with increasing unease and disappointment. Cho Yong-gwan in his recent (2004) academic article catalogues such perceptions, many of which he appears to share: defectors are "impolite," "selfish," and "prone to lies and exaggerations about their past." Citing his own experience and the experience of other people, for example, he complains about the widespread North Korean tendency to invent a great pedigree for themselves or to make up stories. Cho concludes: "The South Koreans initially used to believe that North Koreans, unlike people in a capitalist society, are honest and pure. But when they learned that the Northerners frequently lie, they felt disappointed and began to avoid

---

[23] North Korean official agencies reprinted large articles on the defectors' problems, which were originally published by *Sin Tong 'a* monthly in the December 1995 issue (*Kukmin Ilbo,* June 28, 1999, 5)

[24] See, for example, a recent study (Chŏng 2005) of young defectors' adjustment, dotted with such statements.

interaction with the Northerners" (Cho 2004, 175).[25] He also mentions that there are many cases when somebody "helps the North Koreans a lot, but has his/her own requests completely ignored" (Cho 2004, 174).

In October 2004, the *Tonga Ilbo* daily even considered necessary to publish a special rebuttal to a list of alleged misperceptions about the defectors. The list includes such statements as: "The financial assistance to the defectors is too large," "My tax money is spent on the defectors," "Defectors do not pay taxes themselves," "Defectors are largely involved in criminal activities," "There are spies among the defectors," "Only useless people defect from the North," "What do we get by accepting defectors?" Even though the article's author Chu Sŏng-ha (a defector himself) tries to refute all these ideas one by one as groundless or exaggerated, the very list is telling enough (*Tonga Ilbo,* October 4, 2004, 8).[26]

Quietly Closing the Door:
Seoul's Changing Policy Toward North Korean Refugees

The South Korean government is squeezed between two conflicting imperatives. On the one hand, it is impossible to abandon the long-established fiction of "one Korea" for manifold political reasons. Even the current South Korean government, which is left-of-center and does not share the instinctive anticommunism of earlier South Korean elites, is not in a position to relinquish the myth of unification. At the same time, the bitter experience of Germany, estimates of the economists, as well as the problems outlined here have made the government less than enthusiastic about speedy reunification.

These conflicts can be seen in polling data that suggest a preference for a cautious approach to integration. In late 2004, a public opinion poll indicated that 50 percent of Koreans would prefer "gradual unification" as an ideal scenario while an astonishing 39 percent said that their ideal would be "prolonged friendly coexistence" of two Korean states (in other words, no unification at all!). Only 6 percent expressed their preference for speedy unification ("Kukmin t'ongil yŏron chosa pogosŏ"). President Roh also made clear that the South Korean government should avoid anything that might lead to a regime collapse in the North. He said while in Berlin: "There is a very slim chance that North Korea will suddenly crumble, and the South Korean government is not willing to cause such a situation… Germany paid a high price to realize national unification and is still suffering from it. I hope Korea will not undergo the same" (*Korea Times,* April 14, 2005).

These broader views about unification have crucial implications for South Korean policy toward refugees more generally. First and foremost, the South Korean government has quietly moved away from encouraging defection—and particularly mass defection that might provoke a serious crisis within the North and hasten its uncontrolled collapse. This position became clear in late 2004 when Chung Dong-Young, the Unification Minister, stated that the government is opposing "planned defections" and explicitly emphasized that it has no intention to use the defections to destabilize the North. He also expressed his willingness to crack down on brokers—and such a campaign indeed ensued (*Kyŏnghyang Sinmun,* December 21, 2004).

To appreciate the actual meaning of the minister's remarks about "planned defections," one has to take into account the process of defection outlined above. Since individual defectors are denied assistance by South Korean officials overseas, one needs the help of a professional broker to arrange a crossing to South Korea. Without such help, an aspiring refugee would be unable to contact a Chinese skipper to take him to South Korean waters or acquire the forged passport necessary for air passage. In all probability, the attempt to arrange an independent crossing by somebody without proper contacts and knowledge of the local situation will attract attention of the Chinese police and lead to the arrest and extradition to the North.

---

[25] It is worth noting that disappointment partially results from the fact that North Koreans do not fit into a pre-created, highly idealized image of themselves. Such an image, indeed, has been created by the South Korean left over the last two decades.

[26] The article by Chu Sŏng-ha appeared only in the early issues of the newspaper, but it is available online—explanations about the article provided by Chu Sŏng-ha in a letter to the author.

Thus, any attempt to limit the activity of the brokers effectively means that defection would become considerably more risky or just impossible, which is what the South Korean government apparently wants to achieve by introducing the regulations.

At the same time, the South Korean government cannot openly refuse to accept the refugees since such action would undermine the old claims about South Korea's alleged standing as the sole legitimate government of the peninsula. Hence, its current policy of dealing with the refugees is necessarily hypocritical. Seoul accepts those who somehow manage to get into South Korea while quietly working to make such passage as difficult as possible and steadily reducing the benefits available for defectors. The South Korean government is closing the door in front of aspiring defectors, but trying to do it quietly since an explicit rejection of "brothers and sisters" from the desperate North remains a political impossibility.

Since these concerns are not (and cannot be) openly stated, the official media presents the measures aimed at reducing the number of defectors in purely humanitarian terms. A campaign against "brokers" in 2004-2005 was a good example of such public relations: the campaign was explained away by lofty considerations about the fate of the unfortunate North Korean refugees who are allegedly exploited and misled by the predatory "brokers" arranging for the much vilified "planned defections" (as if staying in a famine-stricken Stalinist country were better for their well-being).[27] The leftist media supported these efforts by publishing articles that described the organizers of the defections as "human traffickers" and by running interviews with North Korean refugees who tell how wonderful–or, at least, tolerable–their life in China is.[28]

Within this context, the resettlement packages have become the target of attack, and are often presented as the major reason defectors come.[29] Indeed, the aid packages paid in the pre-2005 period were large enough to make "chain defections" easy, since the amount of money received by a defector as a lump sum (typically, about $12,000) was sufficient to pay for smuggling another family member and still left some money to survive at least the first few months in the South. The dramatic cut in the lump sum payment in 2005 made this far more difficult and indeed resulted in the reduction of defectors' numbers. In all probability, this was exactly its purpose. Chung Dong-young, the Unification Minister himself, almost openly admitted as much when talking to journalists in late December 2004: "In regard to dealing with the arrivals of the defectors, we also must think how to stop the transfer of their 'settlement money' to the so-called 'defection brokers'" (*Hangyerye Sinmun*, January 4, 2005, 16).

The recent measures were successful, if judged against the government's unstated but clear objectives of reducing defectors' numbers. In 2005, the number of new arrivals was 1,384, against 1,894 arrivals in 2004. The difference is accounted for in large part by the 468 defectors flown from Vietnam. Nonetheless, 2005 would be the first time in recent years that the number of defectors had not increased even if taking into account the Vietnam group. This is not surprising, since in recent years "chain defections" have constituted well over half of the cases, and the dramatic reduction of the initial payment made such defections far more difficult to arrange.

---

[27] See, for example, an interview with a repentant broker, published in the *Hangyerye Sinmun* (December 12, 2004), considered the mouthpiece of the South Korean left: "Only belatedly I realized that planned defections annoy North Korea and China, provoke large-scale arrests of the North Korean refugees living in China, and make more difficult the situation of the refugees who otherwise would live in China or return to North Korea when the economic situation improves." This passage betrays the major desire of the South Korean left (shared by many on the Right as well, albeit with lesser publicity)—to send the North Koreans back to where they belong, to the North, and keep them there. It also contains an implicit denial that the refugees might have any other motivation but an economic one.

[28] The *Mal* monthly, considered a mouthpiece of the more extreme version of the South Korean left, was hyperactive in this campaign. In late 2004 and early 2005, the monthly, widely read by the "progressive" intellectuals, published one or two articles to such an effect in every issue.

[29] Recently, describing the 25 percent drop in the number of refugees after the dramatic reduction of aid packages available to them, a representative of a pro-government South Korean NGO said: "The government has ended the vicious circle when earlier refugees acted as brokers in order to get hold of the 'resettlement money' of new-coming refugees" (*Segye Ilbo*, July 12, 2005, 7). Of course, this "breach of the vicious circle" means that more North Koreans remain in hiding in China, doing odd jobs there—and even more are starving in the North, being unable to overcome the tacit rejection by the South Korean officialdom.

However, there are good reasons to doubt whether the aid package is indeed the major economic attraction for the refugees, outside of the chain-defection mechanism just outlined. Even if money grants and hand-outs to ordinary defectors eventually drop to a purely token level, or disappear completely, migration will be driven by a dramatic difference in living standards between the two Koreas. The gap in living standards between the North and the South is huge: per capita GNP in the South approaches $15,000 while in the North it has been estimated at being between $500 and $1,100. This difference alone, even without the influence of political and cultural factors, makes South Korea a very appealing target for those leaving North Korea.

Conclusion

The last decade has been a time of dramatic change in South Korea's policy toward defectors, as well as in the composition of the defector community. Prior to 1992-1994, defectors were few in number, came from the Pyongyang elite, brought valuable intelligence, and could be easily used for internal propaganda campaigns then waged by the South Korean authorities. The government actively encouraged defection, and showered successful defectors with monetary and other rewards.

However, the last decade has witnessed a change in the nature of the refugees and a quiet reversal of previous policy. The numbers of defectors are growing, but the overwhelming majority of the defectors consist of former farmers and workers from the northern provinces who have spent some time living a precarious existence in China. Typical defectors are not very good at adjusting to South Korean society. The skills that help them survive in the cut-throat world of cross-border smuggling operations and the underground Chinese labor market are not useful in South Korea. Hence, defectors suffer not only from low income, but from real and perceived discrimination, alienation, and the risk of forming a permanent, semi-hereditary underclass. All of these circumstances adversely influence the image of defectors in South Korean society and constitute a vicious cycle of underachievement.

The government increasingly perceives these newcomers as a source of trouble and unnecessary expenditure. Defections are now quietly discouraged, and for a growing number of justifications: to uphold the political stability of the North, to save South Korea's budget, and to avoid confrontation with Pyongyang, whose leaders are clearly sensitive about the refugee issue.

At the same time, the ingrained fiction of "one Korea," enshrined in the South Korean Constitution as well as in the discourses of both Left and Right, means that all North Koreans are technically considered South Korean citizens. This fact greatly limits the freedom of political maneuvering for any administration in Seoul. The South Korean government to a large extent remains a prisoner of earlier nationalist rhetoric and political ambitions of bygone regimes. It has to maintain the fiction of "one Korea" even though the interests of the South Korean public, the sole constituency of the democratically elected Seoul administration, seem to be in collision with the unification rhetoric.

Given these political constraints, the South has adopted a policy of gradual unification coupled with an effort in the short-run to avoid a refugee policy that could have destabilizing effects on the North Korean regime.

In the short run, the current policy aimed at reduction of the defectors' numbers might appear a reasonable, if somewhat cynical, strategy. But in the long run, this policy might have serious side effects that will probably outweigh its perceived benefits. Moreover, an effort on the part of South Korea to shore up the North Korean regime may not in the end succeed. The probability of collapse remains high, whatever Seoul does, and if things take such a turn, defectors will have an enormous social and political significance. For quite a while they will be the only people who will combine a first-hand knowledge and understanding of both North and South Korea. This potentially makes them the major source of personnel for post-unification institutions of all kinds. Defectors could become important interpreters and guides to the outside world, and are likely to be more acceptable to the Northerners than the complete outsiders from the South.

However, the number of refugees in South Korea, and particularly the number of educated refugees, remains too small to play such a role. Therefore, it makes sense to consider a substantial increase in the number of refugees. The current level, which has been stable for the last five years, is about 1,500 new refugees annually. This number is neither sufficient to have a substantial impact on the country, nor to exercise any influence over the course of unification were it to come. The refugee community will start having some impact only if the annual number of newcomers reaches the level of approximately 5,000 to 10,000 a year, enough to generate a critical mass in a matter of few years. After all, this is still well below the level Germany handled on a regular basis for decades, and without too many difficulties.

"Nursing my mother at home. We didn't have money to cover the medical expenses." (China)

Such levels would mean that within a decade or so the total number of refugees will reach the 100,000 mark. To most Koreans this might sound like a very large number, but this is still only 0.25 percent of South Korea's total population. Still, such a community will be large enough to serve as a pool of expertise and also to become, in a sense, self-supporting with connections and experiences of earlier arrivals put to use by later ones. Caring for such a number of new arrivals will cost money, but in the long run their presence will provide insurance with respect to North Korea's reconstruction.

Seoul's political concerns about Pyongyang's reaction to large-scale defection are also not well-founded. Of course, North Koreans will make aggressive and threatening statements about defectors, as they always do. But this is unlikely to have a lasting effect on the bilateral relationship. North Korea takes much more seriously the threat of internal ideological contamination and dissent, and people who have left the country are "spoiled" anyway. It is worth remembering that in the past, South Korea actively encouraged defection, and this policy did not create impassable difficulties for interaction between the two governments. We should also remember that in the German case, the authorities of the communist East learned to accept a far higher level of defections. It is understandable that Seoul does not want North Korea to collapse, and prefers a slow evolution of the regime to a violent revolution. However, supporting defection does not necessarily mean hastening the regime's collapse. On the contrary, such a policy might produce people who will be useful for helping North Korean society to evolve. And if the dreaded collapse happens nonetheless, they will be necessary to sort out its consequences.

To make such a policy work, it is important to take into consideration the social structure of the current defector community and to address some of the problems outlined above. Under the current system, most defectors are unskilled or semi-skilled workers and farmers who are bound to occupy the lowest reaches of the South Korean social hierarchy; this fact alone will remain a source of friction and irritation. Thus, the South Korean government should put greater emphasis on creating a cadre of educated and skilled defectors.

The first solution is to change policy to provide more benefits for those defectors who have education. Elite defection should be encouraged. This might be done through an increase in payments to people who bring valuable information and skills with them. In a sense, elite defection is encouraged now, but clearly with the purpose to obtain more intelligence about the secretive state. However, even if particular members of the elite do not have access to viable political or military intelligence, their arrival should be welcomed.

Another way to change the social composition of the defector community is to provide refugees with more educational opportunities once they arrive in the South. This might be difficult given the current composition of the defector community whose lives have not made them particularly suitable for, and oriented toward, academic achievements, but it is not impossible to pursue a more aggressive policy with respect to vocational education. Even educated North Koreans have at least some troubles in adjusting to the South Korean environment. For example, North Korean engineers do not know how to handle modern machinery and some of them might not even have any experience with computers. This clearly makes them unemployable. It might make sense to consider pilot retraining programs for North Korean professionals whose skills are insufficient or outdated. Experience gained through administering such programs will be of great value in the future when South Korea will face a tremendous task of re-educating the North Korean staff employed by the South Korean companies.

It might also be a good idea to consider an affirmative action program to make sure that at least those defectors who graduated from major South Korean universities and vocational training programs or whose North Korean qualifications are accepted (perhaps, after some re-training) will get reasonable jobs in major South Korean companies and state agencies. Currently, judging by the anecdotal evidence, the major Korean companies avoid hiring defectors. The rumors about such discrimination are very widespread in the defector community. These rumors might be partially or even completely wrong, but they nonetheless have a demoralizing effect on the refugees. If a number of the educated refugees are employed in major companies, it will produce both good role models and skilled personnel for dealing with North Korea in the future, as well as sending a positive signal about the capacity to assimilate.

The international community might have a role to play in this retraining effort as well. Scholarships for academically suitable defectors, especially those in their 20s and early 30s might be a good idea, especially if they choose to specialize in economics and other social sciences and in practical areas of wide significance in a reconstructed North Korea, such as engineering, health care, and education.

It is clear that a large and growing number of South Koreans would be happy to avoid unification altogether, leaving their "North Korean brethren" at the mercy of their fate. The refugees' experience outlined here testifies to the tremendous divergence between the two Koreas. This experience confirms that the unification of the two Korean states will be not only costly, but also socially difficult. It seems that the persistent problems with the refugees' adjustment to their new environment, combined with news about Germany's misfortunes, has further diminished Seoul's willingness to pursue a speedy unification. However, it is neither humane nor prudent for South Korea to turn its back on North Korean refugees. A calibrated policy of increasing the overall number of refugees, encouraging more skilled defectors, and investing intensively in their retraining and integration into South Korean society will at least constitute a worthwhile insurance policy in the eventuality that North Korea either implodes or chooses to open up.

References

Che, Sŏng-ho. 2001. "T'albukja chŏngch'ak chiwon chedo-ŭi silt'ea-wa kaesŏn pangan (The current situation with support of the North Korean defectors upon their arrival and proposals for its improvement)." *Chungang pŏphak* No. 3. Seoul.

Cho, Yong-gwan. 2004. "Pukhan chŏngch'i kyoyuk-ŭi naemyŏnhwa-ga t'albukja namhan sahoe chŏkŭng-e mich'in yonghyang (An influence of the internalization of North Korean political education on the adaptation of the North Korean defectors to South Korean society)." *Hanguk chŏngch'i woegyosa nonch'ong* No. 2. Seoul.

Chŏng, Hyang-jin. 2005. "T'albuk chŏngsonyŏn-ŭi kamjŏngsŏng-kwa nambukhan- ŭi munhwa simlijŏk ch'ai (The emotionality of the young North Korean defectors and the social/cultural differences between North and South Korea)." *Pigyo numhwa yŏngu* No. 1.

Foley, James. 2001. "Ten Million Families: Statistic or Metaphor?" *Korean Studies* No. 1, 96-110.

Good Friends. 1999. *Tumangang-ŭl Kŏnnŏon Saramdŭ*l (People who have crossed the Tumen River). Seoul: Good Friends.

Hamm, Taik-young. 1999. *Arming the Two Koreas: State, Capital and Military Power.* London/New York: Routledge.

Hirschman, Albert O. 1993. "Exit, Voice, and the Fate of the German Democratic Republic: An Essay in Conceptual History." *World Politics.* 45:2.

Kim, Yun-t'ae. Personal interview. March 2, 2005. Seoul.

Kim, Kyu-wan and Pak Sŏng-jo. 2005. *Nam-gwa Puk: Mungch'imyŏn chuknŭnda (North and South: Dead if United).* Seoul: Chung'ang M & B.

Kim, Tong-bae. 1996. "T'albukjadŭl-ŭi chŏkŭng-ŭl wihan mingan ch'awon-ŭi taech'aek (The civil policy for better adjustment of the refugees from the North)." *T'albukjadŭl-ŭi salm.* Seoul: Orŭm.

Kim, Yŏng-su. 2004. "Pukhan it'al chumin hyŏnghwang-kwa chaesahoehwa munje (The present situation of defectors from North Korea and problems of their re-socialization)." *Sahoe kwahak yŏngu* No. 1.

"Kukmin t'ongil yŏron chosa pogosŏ (The report about opinion polls on people's attitudes to unification)." *T'ongil Hanguk.* No. 2. 2005.

Kŭm, Myŏng-ja. Personal interview. March 24, 2005. Seoul

Kwak, I Iae-ryong. 2000. "Pukhan It'al Chumin Ingwon Silt'ae-e Kwanhan Yŏngu (A study of the human rights situation of the refugees who fled North Korea)" *Pyŏnghwa Munje Yŏngu* (The Study of Problems of Peace) No. 1.

Kwak, Tae-Hwan, and Seung-Ho Joo. 2002. "The Korean Peace Process: Problems and Prospects after the Summit." *World Affairs* 165 (Fall).

Lankov, Andrei. 2004. "North Korean Refugees in Northeast China." *Asian Survey* (November-December): 856–873.

Lankov, Andrei. 2006. "Bitter Taste of Paradise: North Korean Refugees in South Korea," *Journal of East Asian Studies* 6:1 (January-April): 105-38.

Lee, Keumsoon. 2006. "The Border-crossing North Koreans: Current Situations and Future Prospects." *Studies Series* 06-05. Seoul: Korea Institute for National Unification.

Ministry of Unification. 2002. *Pukhan it'al chumin poho mit' chŏngch'ak chiwon (Paper issued by the Ministry of Unification on March 19, 2002).*

Ministry of Unification. 2004. *Pukhan it'al chumin ipguk hyŏnhwang (01-04.06) (Paper issued by the Ministry of Unification on July 28, 2004).*

Ministry of Unification. 2004. *T'ongil Paeksŏ (The 2004 Unification White Book).* Seoul: Ministry of Unification, at <www.uniedu.go.kr>

Ministry of Unification, Settlement Support Division, Personal Communication.

National Statistics Office. "KOSIS Database," at <www.nso.go.kr>

Noland, Marcus. 2005. "Political Economy of North Korea: Historical Background and Present Situation." *A New International Engagement Framework for North Korea? Contending Perspectives.* Eds. Ahn Choong-yonh, Nicholas Eberstadt, and Lee Young-sun. Washington: American Enterprise Institute.

Pak, Sang-hak. Personal interview. October 25, 2004, Seoul.

Sŏ, Tong-ik. 1996. "T'albuk kwisun tongp'o ŏttŏk'e ch'orihaeyŏya hana? (How are the defectors from the North treated?)" *Pukhan* No. 5.

Sohn, Kwang Joo (managing editor of the *Daily NK* newspaper). Personal interview. March 8, 2005. Seoul.

Sŏn, Han-sŭng. 2005. *Pukhan it'al chumin-ŭi ch'oeŏp silt'ae-wa chŏngch'aek kwaje yŏngu (A study of North Korean defectors' employment situation and [related] policy goals)*. Seoul: Hanguk nodong yŏnguwon.

Yun, In-jin. 2004. "Kyŏngjejŏk chŏgŭng mullon, namhan saramdŭl-ŭi pyŏngyŏn and ch'abyŏl himdŭlda (Not only economic adaptation, but also biases and discrimination by the South Koreans are difficult [for the defectors])." *Pukhan* No. 9.

Conclusions

Stephan Haggard and Marcus Noland

This collection of essays has examined the plight of North Korean refugees. Estimates of their numbers range from the tens to hundreds of thousands, with the bulk currently residing in China. Although some North Koreans fled to China before the 1990s, the flow of refugees accelerated during the great famine of the mid-1990s. Most of the refugees interviewed by Yoonok Chang and her associates left North Korea because they believed conditions in China were better than those in North Korea. Even with modest improvements in the North Korean economy, increased militarization of the border, and a recent crackdown on refugees living in China, North Koreans continue to leave their country. With the gap between living standards in North Korea and China steadily widening, and with little prospect for significant improvement in political conditions in North Korea, the incentives to migrate will remain high for the foreseeable future.

And these people are indeed refugees. Despite the importance of economic motivations, and the government of China's desire to portray them as "economic migrants," they must be considered refugees on the basis of their well-founded (and well-documented) fear of persecution should they return to North Korea. Few have any intention of doing so. Of the refugees currently residing in China, few would remain there if given the opportunity to resettle, and most would prefer to live in South Korea.

This situation raises important policy issues, most centrally for China and South Korea, but also for the United States, the UN, and other concerned parties. Yet subsequent discussion of the issues confronting these outside actors should not obscure the central point: *it is North Korean government policy—political repression, economic incompetence, and denial of the most basic human rights, including the criminalization of exit—that creates the refugee problem.*

While the fundamental truth should not be lost, there are actions that China, South Korea, the United States, and others can take to ameliorate the refugee problem even if they fall short of a lasting solution.

China

Because China is the first port of entry for the overwhelming share of all North Korean refugees, China's position with respect to them is critical. In policy discussions in the United States, the phenomenon of North Korean refugees in China is sometimes likened to that of Mexican migrants in the United States in order to underline the legitimacy of Chinese concerns. There is some validity in this comparison. In both cases, the gap in income creates strong incentives for migration, incentives that would only strengthen in the absence of adequate controls. In both cases, immigrants provide labor but also confront a variety of social problems and difficulties in being integrated. But the government of Mexico celebrates its emigrants and the remittances they send home; it does not criminalize exit, imprison returnees, or stage public executions of those who help migrants cross the border. Although some sympathy with Chinese concerns is warranted, particularly its concern about a complete collapse of North Korea, we cannot allow these concerns to trump the basic rights of the refugees.

China has fallen far short of its international obligations in this regard. China refuses to permit UNHCR access to the border region, and indeed selectively cooperates with North Korean persecution of its refugees. This has occurred through forcible repatriations, permitting North Korean security forces into China to track down and abduct North Korean refugees, fining Chinese citizens who assist refugees, and detaining and deporting foreigners who assist this population and publicize their plight. China continues to insist, in the face of incontrovertible evidence, that the North Koreans are mere economic migrants. Its obstinacy has blocked what would otherwise be a massive international response in the form of assistance and protection. Moreover, all of this has occurred despite China's membership in the Executive Committee of the High Commissioner's Program and its nominal commitment to refugee rights as a signatory to core protocols.

- Clearly China should uphold its international obligations. One can imagine a three-pronged strategy to encourage it to do so. First is the standard tool of the human rights community: to name and shame.[1] China's refusal to abide by the international agreements into which it voluntarily entered, while maintaining a position of influence within the UNHCR system, is unacceptable. At a minimum, China should allow the UNHCR into the border region and cease its policy of enabling North Korea's depredations. Name and shame has its place.

However morally justified, it is unlikely that appeals to China on the basis of shared values will succeed in bringing its refugee policy into conformity with international norms. As a consequence, it will be necessary to persuade China on the basis of national interest more narrowly construed. One can imagine two sorts of arguments along these lines.

- The first is to appeal to China's growing sense of responsibility and standing in the international community, as outlined in the contribution by Kurlantzick and Mason. China should be reminded that its unwillingness to meet its international obligations has reputational costs. Incumbent powers are likely to resist Chinese initiatives in multilateral institutions, such as the international financial institutions, if it does not meet its obligations in others.

- We must also convince China that current North Korean practices are a threat to its most basic security interests. North Korea's failed economic policies and human rights abuses are not just humanitarian problems: they have the potential to create trans-border public-health problems, generate instability, and generally contribute to a confrontational atmosphere in Northeast Asia.

Yet, however regrettable China's behavior is, it does have legitimate concerns about the presence of large numbers of undocumented North Koreans within its borders, and these apprehensions should be taken seriously and addressed. In particular, North Koreans pose a number of social problems. Since they are unable to work and difficult to integrate, they are vulnerable not only to abuse, but also to the lure of crime and other antisocial behaviors. Politically, Beijing is discomfited about an influx of Koreans upsetting the ethnic balance of its northeast provinces.

- These concerns could be addressed through the establishment of temporary refugee resettlement camps together with third-country commitments to accept the refugees for permanent resettlement. This could be done either through the UN system or on a more ad hoc multilateral basis. Although countries often express reluctance to host such facilities, the management of the Vietnamese boat people demonstrated that such systems were capable of successfully handling large numbers of refugees, at least on a temporary basis. Countries such as South Korea, the United States, and Japan would need to commit to both financing such an effort and accepting refugees for resettlement as appropriate. In the case of the United States, the North Korea Human Rights Act (NKHRA) both clarifies the U.S. commitment to accept North Korean refugees, and in principle makes a down payment on the financing of this commitment. The goal of third-party action should be to make it as costless as possible for China to accept this solution. This is an ambitious vision. It may, therefore, be necessary to persuade China to accept some alternative that would allow the North Koreans to remain in China on a temporary protected basis as an interim solution.

- It is also incumbent on proponents of this approach to assuage Chinese (and South Korean) anxiety that a more formal refugee process is not simply a back-door attempt to achieve regime change in North Korea. China's most basic concern is the potential for instability that a flood of refugees might

---

[1] The tactic adopted by some groups in 2002 to orchestrate entry by groups of North Korean asylum seekers into foreign embassies and consulates successfully turned the international spotlight on the North Korean refugee problem. It also secured transit out of China for a limited number of refugees. However, these incidents also encouraged a crackdown by Chinese authorities, and probably even led directly to the repatriation and deaths of some of those involved at the hands of North Korean authorities. We doubt the advisability of the continued use of this means of attracting attention to the refugee problem.

generate both in China and in North Korea itself. Such concerns are not unwarranted. Hungary's opening of its border with Austria played a catalytic role in the collapse of the East German regime, an historical example with which Beijing (and Seoul) are acutely familiar. Some observers have explicitly argued that opening the door to North Korean refugees could be a route to regime change in North Korea. China (and South Korea), however, are far more discomfited by the potential for instability unleashed by precipitous political change in Pyongyang than they are by the plight of the North Korean refugees. As a result, they are unlikely to reprise the Hungarian role.

However, Chinese cooperation with respect to refugees does not commit it to a weakening of its border security or to any particular strategy toward North Korea.

- There is no reason why Chinese policy could not move on two tracks: upholding its international obligations with respect to North Korean refugees; and continuing its preferred strategy of political and economic engagement with North Korea with respect to the broader security issues on the peninsula.

Temporary resettlement camps are a hard sell, and a certain amount of skepticism about them is warranted. But the current alternatives are worse. As Yoonok Chang demonstrates, the plight of North Korean refugees in China remains bleak. North Koreans entering South Korea increasingly do so through third countries as far-flung as Mongolia, Vietnam, and Thailand. These long, arduous, and costly journeys also exact a major toll on the refugees, both in terms of likelihood of detection and arrest by Chinese authorities, and on their physical health. A number of refugees have died while trying to reach havens beyond China. The imperative is to deal with the refugees in China—their first port of entry after leaving North Korea—not in some other locale.

South Korea

If China's stance has been unconstructive, South Korea's could be described as ambivalent, even shamefully so. Despite its constitutional claim over the whole of the Korean peninsula and its designation of North Korean refugees as citizens of the Republic of Korea, Seoul has been increasingly unwelcoming. The numbers of refugees entering South Korea has increased, although it is still trivial by any reasonable metric. As Andrei Lankov notes in his essay, the total number of North Koreans currently living in South Korea is less than West Germany managed to absorb in a typical year during the Cold War. However, the demographic profile of the refugees has shifted away from elite defectors and as it has, South Korea has become more cautious.

One implication of Chinese policy is that many of the North Korean refugees entering South Korea now do so via distant countries in Southeast Asia or Mongolia. These long journeys are expensive and must be financed in some way. In some cases these journeys are financed by family members or by others connected to the refugees residing in South Korea or other countries, including the United States. However, in the past, the cash award given to North Korean refugees upon arrival in South Korea constituted an important bond, establishing the refugee's capacity to repay debts incurred in passage. The reduction of the cash grant has, in effect, made the commitment to repay less credible.

This change in policy will have two probable effects. The first is to make it harder for refugees to finance their journey, and as a consequence will reduce the number of refugees able to do so. The second is to increase the prominence of criminal gangs—which can serve as an extralegal means of committing to repayment—in the migration process. Unable to avail themselves of the cash bond, refugees are increasingly likely to enter into arrangements resembling indentured servitude to finance their passage. This regrettable situation could be particularly pertinent with respect to women, who have already experienced the depredations of trafficking in their efforts to reach China. Some might object to the implicit use of tax money to finance smuggling networks. However, it would be better to openly recognize that transit over long distances requires real resources and increase the cash awards accordingly rather than to foster even more irregular arrangements.

South Korea also faces challenges in successfully integrating North Korean refugees into South Korean society. On this issue there is opportunity for cooperation with the United States, which has extensive experience with refugee resettlement and integration into the host country's culture. Technical cooperation with South Korea could be a beneficial first step to addressing this issue, and could be particularly important during a period in which the relations between Washington and Seoul are strained.

United States

The United States also has policy obligations with respect to North Korean refugees. Until 2006, the state Department had taken the position that U.S. obligations to North Korean refugees were attenuated because they were in fact South Korean citizens. This stance allowed the United States to sidestep the refugee problem to a substantial extent, with visits by North Koreans to the United States generally limited to speaking tours or special engagements.

The NKHRA accomplished three things: it clarified the eligibility of North Koreans for refugee or asylum status in the United States even if they also qualify for South Korean citizenship; instructed the state Department to facilitate the submission of applications by North Koreans seeking protection as refugees; and authorized up to $20 million per year for humanitarian assistance for North Koreans outside of North Korea.

This is a useful start, but more could be done, particularly on the latter two issues. The legislation calls on the state Department to facilitate North Korean refugee or asylum claims. But the experience of American families attempting to assist North Korean relatives in this process is one of frustration with the disorganization and lack of responsiveness by state Department officials. The state Department needs to task a specific office with implementing the NKHRA refugee resettlement mandate and publicize the relevant contact information throughout the Korean-American community.

Similarly, while the bill authorizes appropriations to support refugees (and other causes as well), the funds actually have to be appropriated through a separate Congressional budgeting process. To date no funds have actually been appropriated for this purpose, although some in the state Department argue that NKHRA has been funded implicitly through other spending.

In short, the NKHRA constitutes a laudable first step with respect to the refugee issue that still nonetheless faces bureaucratic difficulties in implementation. If recent legislation, which passed the Senate as part of the 2007 Defense Authorization Bill, were to pass the House and be enacted, it would require the President to appoint a new Senior North Korea Policy Coordinator. Presumably this individual would be centrally positioned to address shortcomings in U.S. policy toward North Korean refugees.

UNHCR

The UNHCR faces a difficult balancing act. It needs to continue its constructive activities in Beijing on behalf of the North Korean refugees, while at the same time inducing the Chinese government to grant access to the border region. This will almost surely have to come through diplomatic engagement with Beijing by concerned third parties on the UNHCR's behalf. The proposal to take the Chinese government to arbitration over this issue is unlikely to succeed, and could well be counterproductive.

The actions outlined herein—on the part of China, South Korea, the United States, the UN agencies, and other potential hosts—are important first steps in addressing the plight of North Korean refugees. In the end, however, it is North Korea that is central, and it is unlikely that the root causes of the problem can be rectified without significant political change in North Korea. Indeed, it is important to recall that the refugee problem is only the very small tip of a much larger iceberg of repressive conditions within North Korea itself. In addressing the problem of North Korean refugees, it is important to remind ourselves that the task is not simply to improve their lives, but the lives of all the North Korean people.